NOTES OF A FEMINIST THERAPIST

ELIZABETH FRIAR WILLIAMS

PRAEGER PUBLISHERS
New York

Published in the United States of America in 1976
by Praeger Publishers, Inc.
111 Fourth Avenue, New York, N.Y. 10003

© 1976 by Elizabeth Friar Williams

Library of Congress Cataloging in Publication Data

Williams, Elizabeth Friar.
  Notes of a Feminist Therapist.

  Bibliography: p.
  Includes index.
  1. Psychotherapy. 2. Feminism. I. Title.
RC480.5.W47   161.8'914   73-19466
ISBN 0-275-52130-3

Printed in the United States of America

To two cherished models of feminine assertiveness: my mother, Carolyn Loeb Boasberg, and my daughter, Florence Carolyn Williams.

Contents

Preface

This book is intended for all people who are involved in and perhaps troubled by the struggle for new identities and life-styles that engages women today. Women want a change from selves defined by, and · lives organized around, the whereabouts and needs of a Particular Man and The Children. The need for change is clearly indicated by the following anecdote: Four-year-old Missy was watching her mother set the table for guests. Her parents had invited another couple for dinner. Missy walked around the table slowly, carefully counting the places aloud: "One, two, three, four." She stopped. "Oh," she exclaimed, looking up at her mother with enormous, innocent eyes, "aren't you eating with us?"

That's where it's at for too many women, and some of them are painfully examining how they became invisible and what they can do about it. For many women, "what they can do about it" will mean an incredibly complex and difficult journey into territory that has never been mapped for them by society or by other women in their families or social groups. There are, therefore, few models for them among their intimates and there may be even less support. For these women the journey may ultimately involve the dissolution or restructuring of the relationships that currently mean most to them. It may mean not only the discovery of strengths they never knew they possessed but also, for some, the discovery of real limits in their abilities and in their capacity for work as they test out their fantasies in newly available opportunities. For others it may mean the awakening in themselves of sexual appetites they once thought of as perverse. It may mean committing themselves to a formidable educational enterprise, perhaps in middle age. It may mean the decision to have a baby and rear it without a husband, or indeed, to have no children at all and several mates, either serially or simultaneously.

Alternatives like these are so far removed from those that women in our culture have been brought up to expect and to act on that they can scarcely be contemplated seriously as real possibilities without conflict, anxiety, guilt, and insecurity. Fortunately, many contemporary women are finding that they need not confront the pain of change alone. They have invented and are participating in consciousness-raising groups and women's studies programs; they are organizing and joining women's political and professional groups; they have created the need for and provided for themselves career-counseling and educational advisory services, and a unique psychotherapy: "feminist therapy."

In this book I describe those aspects of women's psychological distress that seem to me to be clearly related to their socialization as women in this society. In addition to trying to illuminate what I see as some of the important feminist issues in the psychotherapy of contemporary women, I also describe how a feminist-oriented psychotherapist, whether male or female, uses this perspective to help women in treatment.

I differ from some other feminist-oriented therapists in my contention that not all of a woman's problems are related to her minority-group status and socialization. Indeed, although my focus in this book is on the feminist issues in the psychotherapy of women, I hope I will be able to convey as well my deep belief that all human beings are incredibly complex and by no means yet clearly understood. Any person's behavior gives evidence of an intricate interplay of social, characterological, biochemical, and genetic forces. No one is in a position at this time to say which are the most important of these behavioral determinants. Therefore, I take issue with those who assert that men cause all women's problems or that it is society's negative and discriminatory attitudes toward women that alone cause them to "need" therapy.

The reader will notice that throughout this book I state my opinions and feelings unequivocally and disclose a good deal of information about my own life, past and present. In no sense, then, is this book solely an "objective" work, nor was it my intention to write such a book. The traditional and conventional view is that therapists are and should be detached, remote, "scientific" (as opposed to emotionally involved) and certainly not inclined to reveal much about themselves. This view is changing, however, and many therapists now feel free to disclose who they are to their patients and to a wider public. For me and for my patients, too, it may be as important that I interact with them as the person I am as it is to listen to them disclose who they are.

I felt the same way as a teacher. It was important to me that my students knew the person I was, because I wanted us to be involved with each other in more than a role-playing enterprise, and frankly, because I wanted something from them for myself: I wanted to be regarded as a real person, not primarily as a parent figure who was there only to feed them information about psychology. I wanted to be listened to and to be liked or disliked as myself, not "just" as a teacher, and I recognized and related to many of them also as more than "just" students. (I say "many" of them rather than "all" because some people don't want to be recognized as real, whole persons, preferring to remain safely behind their role masks.)

It became clear to me as I began to write this book that my desire to disclose myself could underscore the book's theme of personal freedom for women, for I wanted to say all through the book, "Hey, it's me talking." I realized that this craving to reveal oneself publicly seems to be quite common among women today. There is certainly a sociological reason for that as there is for so much else about women's feelings and behavior.

It is an essential aspect of women's experience, like that of other "minorities" such as homosexuals, blacks, and Jews, that they often feel illegitimate, as though their needs, their feelings, their physical experiences, and their statements about themselves and their world are not quite so valid as those of the dominant group.* Part of feeling illegitimate is sensing that there are essential aspects of the self that one experiences as shameful and that must be hidden. It is, of course, a crucial goal of any woman's therapy that she eventually feel fully legitimate in all of her aspects. She needs to know that in spite of the fact that her statements may be "wrong" (as men's are often wrong) and although she may act hostile, crazy,

---

*I am greatly indebted to Jerry Croghan for his participation in the development of these thoughts.

stupid, or ignorant at various times (as men also act
hostile, crazy, stupid, or ignorant at various times), she
has as much right as men (or as her parents and children)
to ask for what she wants, to express her pain and ecstasy,
and to make statements about the hostility or lovableness
of other people in her world. She has as much right to say
who she is and how she perceives the world and to say it in
her own way as a man has to state who he is in whatever
terms are comfortable for or characteristic of him.

Many women have only recently discovered the thrill
of revealing themselves through whatever media are
right for them. They need no longer feel ashamed and
fearful of disapproval. That includes me. We need no
longer strive to please others; we need no longer worry
that our individual and group ways of expressing
ourselves are less sane, less valid, less "realistic," or less
respectable than men's ways. These are such new
freedoms and they are freedoms that make us so exultant
that many more women now are saying, as I am: "This is
me, and what I have to say counts! You may not agree
with what I say, you may not like me, and I don't care
(much) if you do or don't. What I most care about is that
you listen to me and take me seriously as I really am and
not react to me as if I'm no more than a concoction of
ideas and roles calculated to please you or to entertain
you or to deceive you about my reality and yours."

The patients whose stories are recounted here are
middle-class, college-educated, white women between
the ages of twenty-two and fifty. None of them is psychotic; none exhibits severe neurotic symptoms such as
extreme obsessional or acting-out or psychopathic behavior. Therefore, they are by no means "sicker" than
people who are not in therapy. On the contrary, their
psychological health is demonstrated by their courage in

seeking what they believe might be radical changes in personality and life-style; by their open-mindedness in attempting a new, unorthodox, politically relevant psychotherapy; and by their willingness to examine and re-evaluate their most intimate relationships as possible sources of their pain.

Acknowledgments

I want to express my loving appreciation to the following friends whose encouragement and provocative insights into women's feelings contributed so much to the pleasure and enrichment I derived from writing this book: Eleanor Ruma, Jeanne Maracek, Marty Seif, Jerry Croghan, Silvia Greenberg, Susan Riemer Sacks, Don Resnick, John Skelton Williams, Jr., Sylvia Gomperts, Bernice Solish, and Nicholas Pastore.

Several feminist colleagues helped me learn that women can be tremendous supports to one another. Carol Gordon, Annette Hollander, Barbara Suter, Betsy Aigen, and Dale Bernstein unfailingly welcomed and contributed generously to my efforts toward personal recognition.

My Gestalt therapists, Dan Rosenblatt and David Altfeld, participated so much in my liberation from old roles and self-destructive attitudes that it would be impossible to enumerate their contributions here. My love for and gratitude to both of them are richly deserved.

Special thanks for their encouragement and lively interest go to my daughter-in-law, Wendy Weiss Friar, my son, Jamie Friar, and my parents, Carolyn Loeb Boasberg and Emanuel Boasberg, Jr.

Writing this book brought me the friendship of two remarkable women: my agent, Helen Brann; and my canny, delightful editor, Gladys Topkis. Complicated, sensitive, and brave in their own lives, they have generously shared their experiences and their competence with me, thus contributing immeasurably to my understanding of women's struggle for respect and recognition and to my own competence and self-confidence. My gratitude to them is indeed deeply felt.

Bruce Tuchman and Susan Leeds were not only skilled and cooperative typists but insightful participants in the development of my thoughts. They helped make work into fun for us all.

ELIZABETH FRIAR WILLIAMS

New York
July, 1975

Notes of a Feminist Therapist

1

What Is Feminist Therapy?

Traditional psychotherapy, which until recently was regarded by many educated people as a support for and agent of personal change, is now viewed by many women as disappointing. The reasons they give for their disillusionment with traditional psychotherapy are diverse.

Some women say that since most psychotherapists, like most other professionals, are male, they may have an emotional investment in encouraging women to continue in traditional male-servicing roles. Furthermore, their goals for women in therapy too often reflect our culture's conventional definition of "normality" for women—for example, the belief that women should be submissive and passive, subordinating their own needs to those of their husbands and children, or that women should resolve their "penis envy" through identification with their husbands and sons and should be able to derive from noncompetitive home-centered activities the same quality of fulfillment that men derive from career success. Since many women are interested in redefining normality for themselves, in seeing themselves in other than home-centered roles, traditional analysis seems to them not to offer much prospect of change.

Other women object to the Freudian orientation of traditional psychoanalysis. The dominant theoretical orientation of many clinicians, both psychologists and psychiatrists, still imposes on female patients models of psychosexual "health" derived from Freud's practice and theories. Freud believed that normal women are sexually less active and desirous than men, that a woman can best achieve sexual fulfillment by producing male children to compensate for her lack of the male organ, that women who do not experience "vaginal" orgasm are sexually immature, and that women's overall sensuality is evidence of their "infantile" and "polymorphous perverse" sexual development. According to Freud, this is most characteristic of animals, prostitutes, and babies, in whom sexuality is "undifferentiated"—that is, not specifically genital—and therefore inferior to men's. Finally, Freud found it unthinkable that a mature, "respectable" woman could desire and enjoy sexual fulfillment outside the emotional context of marriage and motherhood. Today, of course, many people find such ideas old-fashioned and irrelevant.

Many women recognize that, by focusing attention on intrapsychic conflicts as the source of women's psychological distress rather than on societal oppression and prejudice, most traditional psychotherapists increase women's tendency to feel responsible for, and therefore guilty about, their own pain. These self-perceptions inhibit them from engaging in action that would lead to beneficial societal and interpersonal changes.

Some women reject the idea of seeking help from a man. As most nonfeminist-oriented therapists are males, the politics of the therapy room affirms women's lifelong habit of going to male "experts" for advice. Therapy presents one more male authority to look up to, to placate, and to flatter by appealing to his protectiveness and expertise.

And, too, some women are apprehensive about the possibility of sexual exploitation by a male therapist. Many male therapists *have* exploited women patients for their own sexual gratification in the name of treatment; by so doing they have accepted and abused the role of dominant partner in an intimate interaction.

Such attitudes toward psychotherapy reflect the experiences of too many women in treatment, but they are, fortunately, not the only possibilities psychotherapy can offer. On the contrary, contemporary forms of psychotherapy, individual or group, can be an invaluable source of support and self-knowledge for the modern woman in search of autonomy.

Increasing numbers of women who are seeking psychotherapy today are choosing to see a feminist-oriented therapist. This is a therapist who believes that it is healthy rather than neurotic for a woman to explore ways of living that do not primarily involve caring for or "servicing" other people except as a genuine expression of her love for them and *in reasonable proportion to the care and services she arranges to receive from them for herself.*

A feminist-oriented therapist is one who helps a woman to examine how she learned from the culture the behaviors and emotions expected of her as a "normal" woman: behaviors and emotions she now may find bar achievement of her full potential as a competent person and fulfilled lover. For example, a feminist-oriented therapist may help a depressed woman to question whether her condition is the inevitable "result" of the fact that the man she loves does not wish to get married or that she is unable to have children. (Could she not also feel *released* by these circumstances?) A feminist-oriented therapist may ask a patient to question deeply her jealousy of her little sister or young daughter or mother. Is such jealousy an expression of inevitable Oedipal rivalry, as Freud suggested, or might it be the result of overvaluing the attention of the father in her life and undervaluing the potential bond of affection and support among "sisters"? *Must* she feel angry because the man in her life spends more time at work than he does with her? Is there another way to feel than the way she has learned? Could she, for example, feel *pleased* that his need for her is less than she had expected, thus freeing her to develop other, perhaps equally gratifying, interests and commitments to work or to other friends?

A feminist-oriented therapist is one who supports women who want to be assertive in going after what they want in the same way that men do. If a woman wants a high salary, why shouldn't she be encouraged in the "unfeminine" behavior involved in advertising herself, in asking for what she wants, and in competing with others the way men do? If she wants a date with a man, why shouldn't she call and ask for one? (Women have too often been taught that competition is ugly, that their aggression is "castrating" to men, that self-interest is identical to lack of consideration for others. Yet men learn no such negative values about *their* self-assertion; it is considered natural.) A feminist therapist helps her patients to see that those who have defined women as bitchy, castrating, ugly, and selfish when they go after what they want are likely to be men—or women who are themselves afraid of competition. Is it not far more "natural" to be joyfully free in helping oneself to the good things of life than to repress one's desires and capacities in the belief that such self-effacement is "ladylike"?

A feminist therapist believes that a complex life is

possible. If the therapist is a woman with a family she may be living one herself. She need not and should not encourage a patient to follow her specific example, because her task is to help the patient find her own way, but this therapist is, after all, living proof that a woman can be supportive and helpful, involved with the growth and development of others (traditionally "feminine" concerns) and yet at the same time involved with her own intellectual and professional growth, with political issues, and with her economic self-interest (traditionally "masculine" concerns). She may be also an example of how even a "feminist" can enact and be deeply gratified by roles to which she has been culturally conditioned as a woman—mother, wife, homemaker, nurturer. Thus she can help allay the anxiety experienced by many women who want to acquire new role definitions for themselves, yet fear that to do so they must give up entirely some or most of the roles and activities traditionally associated with "femininity."

Specifically, many women are seeking a therapy that is feminist in orientation because

- they want to experience support and guidance from a woman rather than from their traditional experts: men
- they want to grow and to experience their conflicts with someone who has felt the same pain and faced the same dilemmas and who appears to have survived without compromising her integrity as an autonomous adult
- they want a therapist who has no emotional stake in keeping them passive, dependent, and subservient and who does not get sexual confirmation from their admiration or, worse, awe
- they want a therapist who will not appeal to their sexual feelings, who does not tempt them to be

provocative and seductive in the name of "exploring
our feelings toward each other," a does not "get
off" on hearing descriptions of their sexual problems or offer to *show* them how to solve these problems.

- above all, they want a therapist who understands the
role of socialization in creating the attitudes and
feelings that are inhibiting to women's self-
realization and happiness and who will not auto-
matically assume that they are "sick" people who
have come into conflict with prevailing norms as a
result of their pathology

As a feminist therapist, I have goals for my patients
that are directed toward increasing their sense of their
own power, self-esteem, and autonomy. Specifically, I
would like to help women be able to understand the
connection between their conditioning as women and
their present psychological situations—that is, their roles
and the role-behaviors they have chosen to enact. I say
"role-behaviors" because we do not simply choose roles
to enact as the result of our socialization as women; we
also experience certain feelings and attitudes, and we
engage in certain behaviors that are taught to us as
appropriate concomitants of those roles. Here lie our
real problems. For example, it is not only that a woman
has chosen to be a wife or a mother or a mistress or a
secretary that may be damaging to her but that she too
often feels in these roles that she must act as if she has no
power, as if others' welfare must come first, as if she has
less value than the males in relation to her, and so forth.

As a feminist therapist I try to help my women patients
to understand that the self-defeating feelings they experience in the roles they enact are not an inevitable
aspect of those roles. They need not give up wifehood or
motherhood or mistresshood or whatever, but they also

need not cling to the feelings and behaviors in these roles with which they depress themselves, give inordinate power to others, or limit their activities exclusively to those roles. As a feminist therapist I try to understand also that some of my own behaviors and feelings toward my patients may be directly related to my socialization as a woman, and that a particular learned role-behavior— for example, "overprotective mother"—if acted out with a patient, may well be destructive to his or her therapy.

I also try to encourage women patients to seek work that is financially rewarding as well as personally gratifying. I try to encourage women to stay in therapy until they have found a clear direction in terms of a career and until they know that they can perform and enjoy challenging work. One of my definitions of a "healthy" woman is a woman who is able to support herself in work that is fun for her and gives her a sense of competence. If she cannot do this, I consider her therapy incomplete, for if she is unskilled and inexperienced she cannot feel free from economic dependency (and therefore emotional dependency) on someone else.

In sexual and love relationships, I consider it an appropriate feminist goal that a woman be able to experience at least as much satisfaction as she is providing for her partner. If she is putting a lover through school, she'd better be able to ask him or her to do the same for her, if that's what she wants. More than anything, I consider it necessary that a woman feel free to say anything about herself (and about him!) to her lover that she says to her woman friends or to me. If she is intimidated by him and conceals parts of herself, including her perceptiveness about him, because she fears his disapproval, his abandonment, his infidelity, or *anything*, then she still needs therapy. No one should be deprived of the freedom to be fully oneself with a lover. Like flying or fucking or having a baby, this is one of life's great experiences. If she cannot have this freedom with her present lover, she may want to consider a new lover. The point is that she needs to know that she deserves the experience of being herself with her lover, and she needs to know how to go about getting this for herself.

I also feel that it is an appropriate feminist goal that a woman know—and I mean know *exactly* and in every way—how she is making herself available for victimization, if she is. She must see that she almost always has a choice, and, like it or not, she may have to confront aspects of her own acquiescence in her victimhood if she is to feel her true potency. I am not talking about victims of physical aggression, such as rape or mugging. I am talking about emotional victimization. I feel that no woman's therapy is complete unless she is willing to give up whatever "victim" behaviors are keeping her unrealized and frustrated.

Successful completion of feminist therapy, especially with a woman therapist, should help a woman patient to see other women as potential supports and as loving friends at least as desirable and worthwhile as men. She should no longer view other women as second-class citizens or cutthroat competitors for the same kind of security she had always sought (the possession of a man); she should now be free to involve herself in loving and exciting (not necessarily sexual) relationships with other women. In addition to bringing their own rewards, these relationships with valued women may help a woman patient to see her relationships with men from a new perspective, as different but not necessarily superior to her other involvements. That kind of perspective can be among the most liberating she will ever know.

Although I can be hostile toward an individual man when hostility is appropriate, I have little sympathy with a philosophy of sexual separatism or with therapists who support a patient's hatred of men as a group. Sex-role stereotyping is as destructive to men as it is to women, limiting the range of their experiences and the ways in which they can relate to women and to other men. As a therapist who is sensitive to feminist issues, I am nonetheless concerned with helping both male and female patients to overcome stereotyped reactions and behavior. Liberated men and women must be able and willing to help each other overcome role behaviors that inhibit authenticity with the self and each other. I think of feminist therapy as a way to sensitize people of both sexes to the ways in which they use role behavior to keep themselves at a distance from their own and others' realities and from realizing themselves as fully developed human beings.

Can a woman have a successful therapy with a therapist who is not trained as a feminist? Only if she herself is aware of the feminist aspects of her problems and feels secure enough to bring these issues up in therapy and to argue with her therapist if necessary. It can be a useful experience for a woman to have to do this in her therapy. However, if she is fighting the therapist *all the time* about anything, then something is wrong, and perhaps she needs to consult another therapist.

It is theoretically possible for male therapists to be good feminists, but it takes work for them to achieve a real understanding of sexism and its effects on women. Some of the feminist-therapy referral organizations have men on their lists who have taken the time and trouble to go through consciousness raising.

It is important, however, that any therapy, whether by a male or a female, go beyond an appreciation of feminist issues or even sex-role issues in order to provide the most complete therapeutic experience possible for the patient. Sex role isn't everything, and a therapist who insists that attention to only one area will effect a total change in the patient does her an injustice, for she is far more complicated than that.

What about the therapist who is definitely anti-feminist? Can he or she be an effective therapist for a woman? This is like asking whether a patient can have a good therapy experience with a therapist who is anti-humanist. The answer is absolutely no. If a therapist indicates a belief that it is neurotic for a female patient to challenge sex-role stereotypes—if, for example, he or she considers the achievement of marriage and mother-hood as indispensable signs of a patient's health—then this is not a therapist for a woman to see. Other indications of destructive sexism in therapists are detailed earlier in this chapter. (For referral to a therapist who is sensitive to feminist issues, the reader should contact her local chapter of the National Organization of Women.)

2

Love

Many enlightened and liberated women today are seriously questioning the importance that should be placed on love relationships in their lives. They want to know whether there are alternatives to an exclusive relationship with a particular man (or woman); not just theoretical alternatives, but alternatives that can work for them in their real lives. Many women are questioning whether they want a love relationship in their lives at all. Others want to know how their socialization as women affects their opportunities for satisfaction in love relationships. Women are exploring how they can come to terms with the discrepancies between the fantasies of love that nourished and stimulated them as young girls and the realities of love between two adults, each of whom is striving for, among other things, self-realization, a popular contemporary ideal. Some women are wondering whether they will be able to experience sexual excitement without the erotic stimulus of their former masochistic fantasies, which seem so antithetical to their new images of themselves as unbonded and sexually assertive women. Still others are struggling with the question "Can I love someone without deferring to my lover and making myself less important than the other?" The case histories in this chapter and the following chapter on sexuality illustrate a few of the issues and conflicts about love that modern women are bringing to therapy.

As a social scientist trying to formulate some principles regarding human behavior, as a therapist looking for guidelines that might be helpful in my work with patients, and no less as a woman involved in a love affair of my own, I, too, am concerned with these questions, but I have not found and am not sure I expect to find many answers that can be useful beyond each person's unique situation. Like many contemporary women, I believe (or would like to believe) many things about love that seem to be at variance with my own feelings and behavior. For example, although I have long believed that loving relationships with other women can be as rewarding to a woman as relationships with men, until very recently I did not act as if I expected this to be true. I generally sought love, support, and companionship from men rather than women. Although I believe that it ought to be possible for modern women to find gratification in sexual relationships that are not exclusive, I most enjoy loving when investing my eroticism in one "important" relationship. And even though I tell people (and really believe) that some women might be happier if they placed less emphasis on "having a relationship" and being "in love," I myself tremendously enjoy being in love. Thus, although I write in this book and have written elsewhere about the possible destructiveness of the myth of romance for women, I cherish, nurture, and continue to grow through my own romantic feelings. One thing is certain: With regard to problems involving all deep feelings, love among them, people are especially complex—each person uniquely so—and so must be their solutions.

The Need for Approval from an "Important" Man

Many women, once they have embarked on a serious relationship with a man, act and really feel like a "wife" to him, perhaps because they don't have any clearly defined model available to them as "independent woman-in-relation-to-lover." The only way most women know of relating to a male intimate is the way of the "wife."

MARIAN: *"I'll do anything he wants me to."*

Marian is a lovely design student in her early twenties. At the time she entered therapy, she was involved with one of her teachers, Harold, who had been divorced a year earlier. According to his description, Harold had been a "good" husband—that is, faithful to his wife, who had been his first sexual partner. To Harold, as to a lot of men, to be a "man" meant to fuck around, but because he was married early in life he had never had a chance to live out this particular masculine fantasy. Now he felt he deserved this chance. Marian, on the other hand, had incorporated into her value system all the bullshit about what a nice girl deserves and what she "should" have from a man if she's willing to wash his socks and cook his meals. She acted out the role of the good wife, subservient to her man's wishes, sexually faithful, modest around other men, willing to perform the "wifely" chores, and she expected to be rewarded for fulfilling these role requirements by Harold's fidelity and frequent declarations of love. Without verbal assurances of Harold's loyalty, Marian could not sustain a feeling of self-worth.

When she began therapy Marian was depressed and angry with Harold for withholding the assurances of her importance to him that she felt she needed. She was also confused because, like too many young women in our culture, she had been brought up to believe that a woman should give a man most of whatever he wants, and what Harold wanted was less contact with Marian and more dates with other women! Her need to win his approval meant giving up what *she* wanted. He and Marian obviously had different and incompatible objectives at this point in their respective lives. Her dilemma could be resolved only through a long, difficult examination of how she had arrived at the uncomfortable place where she could not feel like an attractive, worthwhile person without constant reinforcement from a man whom she regarded as significant.

It was important for Marian to see that she could survive without Harold's unqualified approval and support. Further, she needed to understand that any independence she achieved would be for her own sake and not in the service of Harold's wish that she demand less of him. A consciousness-raising group as an adjunct to Marian's therapy helped her understand more thoroughly how, by learning only too well her culture's expectations for her, she had acquired, along with womanhood, attitudes and values that were destructive to her self-esteem and that trapped her in a psychological position in which she could only lose.

After many months, Marian was able to recognize and tell Harold that they were at different places in their lives and that she did not wish to continue her relationship with him. She felt (although other people in her consciousness-raising group didn't agree with her) that his need for other sexual relationships was humiliating to her, but more important, she wanted a chance to be free from *any* intimate relationship with a man for the time being so that she could learn more about herself as a woman-on-her-own and could fully appreciate and consolidate her strengths. She was able to leave him only when she became aware that what *she* needed was more important to her than what *he* needed, and that she was capable of supplying herself with the approval and support she formerly sought from men.

From the time they are very little girls, women are encouraged to believe that men's approval and attention will be their only important source of self-esteem, social status, and economic security. This propaganda has at least two seriously damaging effects on women: First, women tend to feel depressed, unattractive, and incompetent if they do not have constant reassurance of their value to a particular man. Second, many women deprive themselves of a comfortable social life, professional esteem, political influence, and economic security for their aging years if they do not have a man to provide these things for them.

This was Marian's psychological state when she began therapy. Like other women who have "lived for" a man, Marian had to reorganize many areas of her life around gratifications and activities that were independent of her love relationship before she could live without Harold as her focus. By working toward the goals of economic self-sufficiency and professional recognition, as well as toward emotional self-support and approval, she began to experience feelings of pride in herself and confidence in the future that she never before had known or could expect to know as a "lady-in-waiting."

Loss of Identity in a Lesbian Love Affair

GWEN: *"I don't know who I am any more."*

Gwen is a beautiful professional woman in her late twenties. Although she had had a few sexual relationships with men, she felt most involved emotionally and sexually when her lover was a woman. When she first came to therapy she was extremely depressed and anxious about her relationship with Alice, a woman who had been her lover for a year and with whom she was sharing a summer house. There were a number of value conflicts between Gwen and her lover. For example, Alice was anti-"professionalism," while Gwen derived a great deal of self-esteem and pleasure from the knowledge that she was skilled and respected in her profession. Alice thought Gwen's involvement in her work indicated a slavish identification with "middle-class" values, and because Gwen was much concerned with and influenced by her lover's opinion (even though in other situations she could be extremely independent and strong-minded), she felt unsure of her convictions when criticized by Alice. She grew doubtful about the motives underlying her love of her work and about its importance to her.

Gwen and Alice also had different opinions about so seemingly trivial a matter as taste in clothes. Gwen was unusually attractive and very well paid. She liked to wear pretty clothes and could well afford them. Alice felt that this interest in clothes was too "feminine" for a homosexual woman and, again, too frivolous and "middle-class." She tried to make Gwen feel guilty for caring about clothes, and once again Gwen allowed herself to be vulnerable to these criticisms and became inhibited about expressing good feelings about herself by dressing attractively. Thus she almost completely deprived herself of two important sources of self-esteem for *her* (although admittedly not for everyone): her work and her appearance. Gwen's depression can be explained in part by this depletion of pride in herself.

Her suppression of areas of interest with which she strongly identified made Gwen begin to feel as if she were, in her phrase, "merging" with Alice, but not in the positive sense in which the word is usually intended. She could no longer feel secure about who she was. She felt overwhelmed by her lover's ego boundaries (identity) and diminished as a separate person. Gwen was anxious as well as depressed because her discomfort forced her to think about separation. Realistically she felt that this particular relationship, or at least her reaction to it, was destructive to her, but she was also very much attached to Alice and believed she was more dependent on her than it turned out she really was.

In spite of her emotional discomfort, the first day Gwen came to therapy she appeared very controlled and "together": attractive, poised, and articulate. She placed a great deal of value on "being in control," and this turned out to be one of the ways she lost contact with herself. Through "control," Gwen shut herself off from self-awareness, walling off her most tender and passionate feelings because she feared that by revealing emotion, particularly distress or need, she would suggest to others and to herself that she was incapable of putting her affairs "in order" (as if "order" were a possible or even a desirable state for human affairs to be in). She came across to herself and to others as vague, as if she did not have a vivid and unique personality. An unfortunate consequence of her undue self-control was that it discouraged gestures of warmth and support from her friends and colleagues. Gwen's manner convinced her associates that she was capable of "taking care of herself" when, in truth, she desperately wanted and needed to feel others' interest and warmth. (Unfortunately, like many women, Gwen felt guilty about being an ambivalent, sensitive, emotional human being and felt inferior to the ridiculous and inhuman model of emotional detachment offered by many men.)

One of the things Gwen was most concerned about, and understandably so, was whether I, as her therapist, would share the opinion of much of the psychiatric world that people who live in homosexual relationships are "sick." She had hoped that a feminist therapist would be able to depart from traditional ways of looking at homosexual problems, if for no other reason than that she is a member of an unconventional group herself and should have worked through her own qualms about being different. Unfortunately, many women therapists who are not feminists have attitudes toward male and female homosexuality that are no more liberated than those of the male psychotherapy "establishment." These attitudes reflect society's fear and disapproval of "deviant" behavior of all sorts, as unwelcome and frightening challenges to the status quo. When members of a "minority" group, such as women therapists, identify uncritically with the dominant group they can become fierce oppressors of people whose very conditions of oppression they share.

Gwen's choice of a feminist therapist also reflected her anger toward and distrust of men, particularly her distrust of men's sexual interest in her. Seeing a woman therapist would eventually present other problems for her, some of them sexual, but that prospect was not nearly so difficult for her to contemplate as trusting a man to treat her with respect.

Although Gwen is what society calls a deviate because she prefers a homosexual love relationship, the problem she presented is one suffered by many people in heterosexual relationships. Gwen had other problems more directly related to her homosexuality, but those were not the ones causing her the most intense anguish, nor did I, as her therapist, feel that her homosexuality was in itself a reason for her to seek psychotherapy. I believe, however, that her sensation of loss of identity may have been intensified because she and her first partner were of the same sex, although they were certainly different in most other ways. It is also possible that because Gwen felt guilty about and ashamed of her homosexuality at the time she began therapy, she thought of herself as having little right to assert her own needs and values. If there was "something wrong" with her, she reasoned, did she deserve to assert her identity vigorously?

A feeling of identity loss in a love relationship usually occurs when one partner "gives up" activities, friends, or attitudes that he or she genuinely values and finds gratifying in an attempt to identify with those of the loved other. Sometimes people do this because they think it enhances a state of "romance" to be so merged with one's lover, but more often people in love abandon their uniqueness because they fear the loss of approval that might ensue if they maintain their differences from the lover. Furthermore, for reasons that are not yet completely understood, some people seem to be more sensitive than others to "separation anxiety." (Perhaps as infants they had poorer "mothering" or more traumatic early separations from loved ones than other babies.) To such separation-sensitized people, merely to assert one's differences from a lover may imply the possibility of a separation that is perceived as catastrophic. To be close to a lover and yet maintain a sense of one's distinctiveness is a critical problem in many people's lives, one that is almost never resolved once and for all but with which most lovers must struggle most of the time they are together.

Women may be more likely than most men to suffer

the anxiety of identity loss in a close relationship because a woman is actually expected and trained to derive her identity from her partner, just as, when she was growing up, her whole family derived its "identity" (social status and community "image") from the father's reputation and social position. It seems plausible that as women pursue without guilt careers and interests that are independent of their family's and partners' needs, values, and physical presence, they will be better able to sustain intimacy without the fear of losing their sense of themselves as unique beings.

By examining her lesbianism with her therapist and by releasing herself from feelings of inferiority and guilt about it, Gwen was able to accept some of her other needs and values as worthy of her own support and that of her lover, whoever that might be. After some time she realized that Alice was too possessive and too denigrating for a happy relationship to develop. When she became more secure, she was able to leave this unsatisfactory relationship, which had been so threatening to her perception of herself as a whole, worthwhile, and separate person. For a while she lived happily alone, making many new social contacts that would have been discouraged by Alice. In a few months Gwen formed a much more satisfying relationship with a woman whose values were more like her own than Alice's and who also was more tolerant and supportive of those of Gwen's interests and involvements that were different from hers.

The new lover was not insulted or threatened by Gwen's need to see herself as a separate person and so had no desire to pressure Gwen into assuming an identity that was not her own. At the same time, Gwen achieved enough self-esteem to be able to take the risk of vigorously asserting her right to be different. Frequent assertions of her identity and her differences from her lover, whenever she felt them to be appropriate, contributed to Gwen's confidence in the integrity of her unique personality.

It should also be noted that Alice had shown that she did not have a clearly defined sense of *her* separateness from Gwen, for she acted as if Gwen were an extension of herself, in the manner of a controlling, possessive mother, another role to which many women are socialized. She was not responsive to Gwen's efforts to point out and change the ways by which she contributed to Gwen's distress, even though these changes might have made her happier, too, in their relationship.

The Myth of Romance

REBECCA: *"I want a* real *relationship, not the one we have now."*

Rebecca, thirty years old, came to therapy after separating from her husband. They had a daughter who was then six months old. Although she had worked as a teacher before her marriage, Rebecca had hated teaching and had regarded it as "something to do" until she married. (When she did marry she gave up work immediately.) Early in her therapy she complained bitterly about everything that didn't go her way—the difficulties of raising a child alone, the problems divorced women have making ends meet on a limited income, how hard it is to get adequate child care, and, needless to say, how hard it is to find what she most wanted: an "intense, long-lasting, and involved" relationship with a man. When she left her husband, Rebecca had many fantasies about the kind of life she would live without him. For example, she thought it would be "fun" to live alone with her daughter; they would enjoy each other without daddy around to make demands on either of them. She thought she would easily find a part-time job writing or doing the creative work she liked. Best of all, she thought she would have little difficulty finding an exciting love life, for she was aggressive and attractive, had been popular before her marriage, and had many friends who could probably introduce her to available men. She also had an intense sex drive and felt sure that this motivation would "somehow" lead her to a satisfying lover.

Her first affair after her divorce was with a much younger, very attractive, spoiled, and narcissistic man. He wasn't everything she wanted, but he *was* unattached. However, Rebecca found that if she paid attention to all of his childish needs she became a mother to *two* children and could count on very little emotional support for herself. Where were those attractive and supportive male intimates she had expected to find?

While she was looking, she was resentful of and angered by the baby's demands for her love, care, and attention, for she could not find the love, care, and attention that she wanted for herself. Indeed, far from having an exciting and "fun" time with her little girl, Rebecca found that when mothers and infants are together for long periods of time they tend to get on each other's nerves; yet she found it difficult to arrange relief. Because it was she who had left her husband, Rebecca felt "responsible" for the failure of her marriage and guilty toward her husband, who, indeed, enjoyed his role of "injured party." Because of her guilty feelings she could not bring herself to ask him to take the child more often than once every two weeks or to contribute more money (which he could afford) so that she could hire a regular sitter. (For all the men who bitch about paying alimony and child support to women whose culture never prepared them for self-support, there are at least as many women who are too ashamed and guilty about the "failure" of the marriage—which they perceive as their personal failure to maintain family harmony—to ask for a reasonable amount for themselves and their children!) Rebecca's fantasies of a quickly established new liaison that would be "intense, long-lasting and involved" were hardly realistic, but they were not evidence of "emotional disturbance," for all women in our culture are taught that they should expect love and protection from a man, no matter what the reality of their circumstances, such as their age and access to men, and regardless of whether there will be men available for them who are capable of being satisfying partners. Nothing in Rebecca's conventional upbringing prepared her for the fact that she might *want* to reject the men who would one day be available to her, preferring to live alone or even to relate as an *equal* partner to another woman or to a man.

As she began to recognize that no fantasy-man was on the horizon and that she could not survive if she merely played at working until rescued by a man, as her culture had promised her, Rebecca brimmed over with perfectly understandable resentment because she felt she had been victimized by society's false promises.

Eventually she was able to assess the real obstacles she faced, obstacles that existed not because there was anything "wrong" with her but because her life as a divorced mother with an infant, in realistic terms, couldn't be easy. She was going to have to get training for a profession other than teaching, which she truly detested, and to stick with it until she could make a better living. If she wanted to live comfortably and have some time away from her daughter's company, she was going to have to scrounge for baby-sitters and be able to pay them. She would have to go to school, and then she might have to work hard for long hours away from home in a field where an income was assured.

Eventually she found a lover she liked, even though he

was far from being her fantasy-man. He had only recently left his wife and children, and Rebecca discovered that
she, like Marian with Harold, wanted to see him much
more often than he wanted to see her. Furthermore,
because she had a young daughter and it was hard for
her to get out, she wanted him to visit her on their dates
while he, on the contrary, was enjoying his new freedom
and liked to go out or to have her come to his own new
home. These realities were some of the sources of fric-
tion between them.

Before therapy Rebecca saw herself as *uniquely* deprived. She had learned through her socialization to
expect to have a thoroughly lovable man and a protected
life served up to her. She now complained about her new
boyfriend and complained and complained. She said she
wanted a "real relationship, not the one we have now."
She was absolutely stunned when she realized in therapy
that a *real* relationship was exactly what she had, and that
what she had learned to expect was a *fantasy* relationship.
Where did she think this was going to come from? Who
was there available to fulfill this fantasy? How did she
think a "real relationship" developed between two people? And how, realistically, could she find the time away
from her daughter's needs for mothering and the
energy, after school and work, to look for and work
toward an even moderately gratifying relationship,
much less a perfect one?

This story certainly has no happy ending in the style of
romantic fiction and our culture's promises to women.
Rebecca's therapy didn't bring her a wonderful man who
is now supporting her financially and devoting his emotional life exclusively to her. Her therapy, however, had
other rewards. She became much less depressed because
she recognized that, though she was indeed a victim, her
position was not due to any particular neurosis or
shortcoming of her own. Rather than feeling uniquely

deprived, she saw that her entire sex had been victimized by the same kind of unrealistic preparation for life that characterized her own upbringing. Recognizing the fraudulence of the romantic goals of her childhood, she was relieved of a sense of guilt and of inadequacy for not achieving them; she could then mobilize her considerable energy in the service of starting from where she was, not without bitterness but without debilitating cynicism, hopelessness, and feelings of inferiority. Another result of her therapy was that she developed enough freedom from guilt to ask her ex-husband to take a much larger share in caring for and financially supporting their child.

Rebecca's situation at the time she entered therapy illustrates very well the complex interplay of social forces and a woman's unique responses to them, which contribute to her suffering. Frustrated by her inability to realize her fantasies of a man's love and protection, Rebecca, like many women, blamed her own inadequacies rather than society's unrealistic expectations for her.

The difficulties Rebecca experienced after she left her husband confront many thousands of women who, for whatever reasons, are no longer happy in their marriages and are ill prepared psychologically and educationally to sustain themselves without a husband. Now, it may be that Rebecca's decision to leave her marriage was premature; perhaps it was related to a pattern that seemed characteristic for her—that is, making something that didn't conform to her fantasies seem unendurably disappointing and victimizing. With such a construction she might well have left indignantly (as she did) without letting herself fully experience the importance to her of her loving feelings for her husband. If she had been in therapy during the time of her early marital difficulties, she might still have decided to leave, but she would have known better what kinds of feelings to expect in herself away from her husband and also might have been better prepared for some of the disappointing and frustrating experiences that invariably confront divorced mothers. This is a situation that often requires great courage, stamina, self-knowledge, and tolerance for discomfort. Therapy can help a woman realize these strengths in herself while at the same time affirming, where appropriate, her perceptions of her suffering as unfair and in great part the result of the inadequate preparation for self-support that is afforded to women in this culture.

Most of us, women and men alike, grow up believing at least two popular myths about love. One is that if only we had had the "right" kind of love from our parents we would inevitably be happier and more successful than we are; the other is that "long-lasting, intense, and involved" relationships are available for all adults who are "healthy" enough to pursue or to be receptive to them. In spite of what some psychologists and others say, long-term, loving, sexually satisfying relationships are probably not readily attainable for everyone who wants them. Therapists in practice know many disappointed people who believe that psychotherapy will or should result in the magical personal transformations that will lead to such a relationship.

Women especially have been encouraged to believe that permanent (married) love is the reward of perfect, approval-seeking little-girlhood, while men have been taught to expect power and affluence as the reward of perfect competency-seeking little-boyhood. Even now, with divorce rates at an all-time high, few people seriously question whether a life-long, exclusive, married love affair is even a desirable goal for anyone, male or female, and young girls are still expected to live out the notion that future married love is the only focus around which to organize all their developing feelings and skills! Therefore women who have not achieved such a relationship come to therapy (and to other sources of consolation, personal change, or oblivion) believing that they *should* feel totally depressed, inadequate as human beings, worried about their "neuroses" or "inability to make contact," dissatisfied with their appearance, and hopeless about their chances for future happiness and personal security.

Another problem that confronts a woman who hopes to fulfill her romantic fantasies is the precipitous decline in the number of men available for her after she reaches her late twenties. To be sure, men die earlier than women, but that's not the only reason men are scarce for the "older" woman. Equally significant is the fact that men are culturally conditioned to fall in love with and to seek as wives women who are younger than they are.

One problem for a woman in a romantic relationship that is of particular interest to feminists is that her acculturation into the servicing role of "wife" has been so complete that she can scarcely relate to one male intimately over a long period of time without deferring to him in countless ways, both consciously and unconsciously. The moment she attaches herself in a committed way to a man, a woman in love often begins to see herself as society sees her—that is, as inferior to him.

Ironically, we teach little girls that marriage is the best thing that can happen to them when they fall in love, when in reality it may be the worst. Not only does my experience with patients and my own common sense tell me this, but recent sociological research indicates that contemporary marriage, although it is good for men, may well contribute to women's physical and emotional disabilities. If a modern young woman in love has the social independence to resist everything she's been urged to revere since she was a tiny child, she'd probably be well advised not to settle in with a man she loves at least until she has developed an independent identity and income and learned to establish and maintain meaningful and loving (not necessarily sexual) relationships with other men and women. By that time she may recognize that by living with the man she loves, as his wife or "wife," she may well lose more than she could gain.

Love Affairs with Father Figures

WINNIE: *"I need help in getting out of my affair with Howard. I still feel mesmerized by him."*

Winnie came to New York to enter graduate school about a year before she started therapy, at the age of twenty-one. New to the city and to the demands of graduate study and always shy with her peers, she found herself overwhelmed by anxiety regarding her ability to make friends and compete for adequate grades. It was the custom of her department to assign small groups of students to various faculty members to meet regularly as work teams so that the students could practice carrying out research projects. Each group met under informal conditions in the members' homes and soon, through close contact and shared goals, emotional intimacy developed among many group members. In some cases, of course, this intimacy extended to sexual relationships.

Howard was a research professor whose small group included Winnie. Howard was frustrated in two ways. First, when he himself had been a graduate student in the same department, he had been the "fair-haired boy" of the department chairman, a distinguished senior scholar. Now in his early forties, with many publications to his credit, Howard had virtually no chance of being promoted to department chairman until the still far-off retirement of his famous colleague. At the same time, his work was constantly and not often favorably compared to that of his chairman, for Howard had chosen to follow the same program of research that the chairman had innovated many years before.

Second, Howard was frustrated by changes in his wife. Now that their children were adolescents she had decided to take advantage of the university courses available at her doorstep and was on her way toward an advanced degree. No longer exclusively dependent on Howard for intellectual stimulation or companionship, she aroused feelings of insecurity and resentment in him. He was no longer going to be the only one she relied on, whose word she respected, whose advice she followed. Moreover, she wanted much more free time for herself, and for the first time she requested his help in getting meals together for the family or in entertaining the kids on weekends while she studied or met with her fellow students. Obviously there were now tremendous shifts in their ways of perceiving each other and in what they needed from each other.

In classic fashion, a relationship developed between Howard and Winnie that resembled the earlier stages of Howard's relationship with his wife. His characteristic pattern in meeting challenges was to take the easiest way. It was apparently easier for him to fall into a "new" relationship that required no real changes in him than to participate with his wife in the difficult soul-searching that might lead to a new relationship between them or to a mutual decision to divorce.

Howard was probably attracted by Winnie's insecurity as much as anything else about her except perhaps her apparent willingness to accept him uncritically. When she was not in his presence she often expressed dissatisfaction and hostility toward him; when with him she suppressed her realistic criticisms in order to please and flatter him. She correctly perceived his insecurity and defensiveness, but her fear of challenging him never gave either of them a chance to discuss these realities.

Winnie came to therapy in great distress; she felt hooked by her "need" for Howard, yet his attentions had not made her less anxious or better able to relate to her peers. As a second-year student, she still had exactly the same social and academic problems that she had had when she first started her graduate work, with plenty of additional tensions. Now she was in a demanding intimate relationship with a man who had increasing troubles in his own family. She was only twenty-two and had no familiarity with the sexual and emotional problems of middle age and an unhappy marriage, such as her lover was experiencing. Winnie allowed her difficult relationship with Howard to consume most of her time and psychic energy, and this further removed her from potentially rewarding contacts with her peers. Her tendency to isolate herself from other students exacerbated their distrust of her; they saw her isolation as rejection of them and her involvement with one of their teachers as threatening to them.

In small, intensely competitive departments, students often vie with one another for the favorable attention of their teachers, whose personal interest can often mean better references for jobs, more help in negotiating a thesis through committees, and so on. A student's love affair with a teacher arouses anxieties and rivalries in the teacher's other students, who are often correct in sensing the competitiveness of a student who cultivates the teacher's attention. Furthermore, some students feel anxious at the breakdown of traditional Oedipal boundaries. In a similar situation of which I know personally, the teacher in question was prevented from being promoted to a full professorship by a graduate-student screening committee whose approval was needed for all promotions within the department. Several of the student members had worked closely with him and had been upset and angered by his affair with one of their fellow students the year before. These students' unresolved feelings of rivalry and rejection and their anxiety at this boundary-blurring in a "family-romance" situation had never been dealt with adequately and resulted in behavior toward the professor that was punitive and irrelevant to his academic adequacy.

There are obvious feminist issues in this story. The attraction of Winnie and Howard for each other falls into the traditional man-woman power arrangement, one that is often eroticized during the Oedipal stage in a young girl's development: the uninhibited, sexy little girl and her father seduce each other partly by suggesting that each can supply what the other lacks. The little girl wants power, which, she is taught, she must get only through a man's approval, not through her own efforts at independence and competence. The father wants assurance that he is important, wonderful, and worth seducing, which he no longer gets from his too wise (and by now, perhaps, too hostile) wife.

Many, perhaps most, little girls, like Winnie, never develop feelings of competence outside the sexual arena. When thrown into a situation that demands more adjustment than they can manage at a given time, they fall back on the only skill they think they have in order to achieve the only security they were taught to seek: the sexual attention of daddy. In a business, academic, or political organization, where arbitrary hierarchies exist, those who have status or power are clearly labeled daddies: boss, president, dean, professor, congressman, mayor, and so on. Naturally the "little girls" head for them. Of course, people thus labeled are almost always men, and needless to say they are in great demand as lovers by women who may feel impotent themselves but are attracted by the power certain social roles imply. The opposite is also true, of course. As women therapists and professors know, "little boys" fall in love with them, too, particularly those who for one reason or another despair of achieving power themselves.

My version of the Oedipus Complex is that sexual possession of the parent of the opposite sex is not so important an issue as approval from the powerful figure. Before they go to school the little boy and girl think that mother, who bosses them around and takes care of them, has the power. Both want her love and approval and are "in love" with her. Pretty soon they get the real picture. It's daddy who's got the power or who is supposed to have it. Now both give up their fascination with mother and start cultivating the approval and attention of father and other males. The boy doesn't have to eroticize his attachment to his father because his father's approval comes from the son's being like daddy, not from seducing him. The opposite is true for the little girl. What turns her on is the sense of power she gets from daddy's approval of her sexuality. (He certainly doesn't approve of her brains or independence.) For too many women, that's the only thing about themselves they ever value. They never learn they have anything else. For many women the so-called repetition compulsion of the Oedipal years—the need to seduce father figure after father figure in order to feel powerful and alive—is the consequence of never feeling alive or competent in any other function.

Among the most important adjuncts to Winnie's individual therapy was her participation in a consciousness-raising group and in weekly group therapy. She very much needed and wanted the experience of trusting others who had equal status in a group setting, and she needed and wanted to learn how to enlist their approval and support for those of her skills and endeavors that were nonsexual. She was relieved to find friends outside her school situation who had no vested interest in her relationship with Howard and could respond to what she said about him as if he were just another man, not an important professor. It was refreshing for her to think about him in this way, without the aura of prestige that surrounded him at school, where she found it so difficult to overcome her awe of him that she couldn't assert her needs in their relationship.

The new trust in others and new skills in making friends that Winnie derived from her work in the therapy group carried over into her school relationships. She found that she became less interested in Howard as she was more accepted by her peers, and she decided that her chances of growing more secure and independent would be better if she were not in a relationship that so readily evoked all her old baby ways of reacting to and dealing with men. (When she was with Howard, for example, she found herself much more likely to cry, to become inarticulate, and to feel helpless and sorry for herself than when she was in either her consciousness-raising group or her therapy group.)

Winnie's experience of her sexuality changed remarkably. In the therapy group she found it possible to feel sexy toward men who did not have a need to see her as a little girl dependent on their "strengths," and that was a tremendous revelation to her. She reported that her sexual fantasies changed from those where she sat on the man's lap and "let" him fondle her to those where she actively seduced a man into satisfying *her*. Before it had been all for him (or so she was taught to believe).

She soon found a boyfriend among her classmates who was more able to adapt to her new independent self than Howard had been. Winnie could then see the difference between the fantasy of feeling secure because a "prestigious" man paid attention to her and the reality of feeling

secure through trusting in and exercising her compe-
tencies independent of a man's approval. In addition,
Winnie could understand and be helpful with the problems of her new boyfriend because they were similar to
hers: anxiety over schoolwork, looking for a job, getting
together a thesis outline. Howard's problems had been
unlike hers, and she could do little to help him deal with
them. Thus she could feel much more like a potent
contributor to her new friend's development than she
could with Howard, to whom she was primarily a little
girl sex-partner, not a mature life-partner. In turn, the
new lover could participate much more fully in her life
and development than could Howard, with his many
other commitments and anxieties.

Winnie changed a great deal, and her life changed a
great deal during her therapy. I think there are several
reasons for this, which certainly do not apply in all cases.
First, Winnie was young and attractive and intelligent.
These qualities drew people to her initially so that she
had a large pool of potential friends if she wanted them.
Second, she was willing to expose herself to two intense
social "laboratory" situations in addition to her relationship with her therapist: the consciousness-raising group
and group therapy. These learning experiences broad-
ened her perspective about her relationship with Howard and provided her with an opportunity to observe
herself interacting with others. She learned exactly what
she did to attract people and how she pushed people
away in certain circumstances. She attained much more
confidence in her ability to get what she wanted from
others and reject what she didn't want.

BRENDA: *"Joel feels threatened by my schoolwork."*

Brenda grew up in a family that highly valued

academic achievement (for men). Her father was a professor in a famous medical school and was also respected as a skilled clinician. Brenda's only brother became a doctor. Feminists will sigh in sad recognition as I say that Brenda, although Phi Beta Kappa at college, decided that she would become a technician in a chemical laboratory when she graduated. Although extraordinarily bright and skilled in the kinds of subject matter that make up a pre-med college curriculum, Brenda found it unbearable to contemplate potential equality with her father and brother by studying medicine.

Brenda was an Oedipal daughter. At the time she entered therapy, in her fifties, she was very much attached to her father, who had just died, and she greatly overvalued him. It was impossible for her to see him in perspective as a human being whose values and manner were not above criticism. During her early life Brenda had lived only to please him and to gain attention from him. It had never occurred to her that she might ever want anything more than her father's approval. It goes without saying that she was intensely competitive with her brother and sisters and with her own mother, all of whom vied for daddy's recognition and for a piece of his off-call time, which he rationed very frugally.

Like many daughters whose relationship with a distant and awesome father is greatly romanticized, Brenda felt most erotic in the company of men who were somewhat distant from her and whom she respected for their intellectual "brilliance" and status. If she felt equal to a man she lost her sexual interest in him, although they might still be good friends. It's not surprising, therefore, that she fell in love, during her junior year, with the young medical student who was the lab assistant in her biology class. After her graduation they married. Eventually her husband, with her considerable support, became an important scholar and clinician in the same field of medicine as her father.

When Brenda first came to therapy she spoke of her husband in exactly the same way she spoke of her father. It was clear that she was "in love" with both of them. Her husband, Joel, was "always right" and "only wanted what was best" for her, even if that meant forbidding her to go to evening classes or to see friends on her own. It seemed to him that Brenda was only happy taking care of his needs and that for her to aspire beyond her "real" talents would "disturb" and "exhaust" her. This is what he told her.

Her father's death came at exactly the "wrong" time for Brenda to recover from it easily. Her oldest children were away at college, quite grown up and able to care for themselves. The youngest child was in high school, but he was much involved with his friends and extracurricular activities and left his mother little to do for him other than make his sandwiches early in the morning. Often he didn't return from his after-school activities until long after dinner. In addition to recognizing that she was no longer needed by her children, Brenda was also at this time experiencing menopausal discomforts.

Essentially Brenda was a bright, intellectual woman with strong achievement needs. She was really going crazy with boredom trying to make a day's work out of the few fancier domestic jobs that the maid didn't do, such as baking and freezing hors d'oeuvres and needlepointing rugs and pillows—hardly satisfying achievements for a smart woman. Her feeling of chronic dissatisfaction at the little she bit off to chew was expressed in part by her need to nibble constantly at the food in the refrigerator. Daily life for her was like trying to exist on a diet that was not only inadequate but bland. She needed much more challenge to give her a feeling that she was engaged in something worthy of her energies and appropriate to both her talents and her values. Like most of us, Brenda had been trained to value the kinds of achievements that only boys are actually expected and encouraged to seek. Therefore, she was always "hungry," like all people who, for one reason or another, do not achieve goals that they value and that they have the mental capacity, if not the opportunity, to achieve.

Brenda's dilemma is one that often brings women to psychotherapy (even without the additional psychological distress of the recent death of a beloved father): the fear of success. As capable and as achievement-oriented as her husband, Brenda feared that if she achieved goals that would make her "equal" to him she would lose her sexual interest in him, for she experienced her romantic awe of him as powerfully erotic. She was indeed "in love" with him, as she had been with her father and other long-ago male authority figures. It seemed to her that her sexual pleasure was dependent upon keeping herself somehow "inferior" to a man she could then "adore."

This view of the fear of success is a little different from that of many feminists who believe that women keep themselves "unequal" in order to please men who they fear would reject them if they were perceived as equals and therefore threatening to men's power-in-the-world. My view gives no less responsibility to the woman who keeps herself down than to the man who may refuse to "give" her the time, money, and emotional support to pursue achievement outside the home. Where the woman has a strong erotic attachment to her "inferior" status in relation to men in general or to a specific man, it may be more than usually difficult for her to give up her "inferior" position. Sometimes such a woman becomes her husband's or lover's associate and finds a good deal of intellectual stimulation and emotional gratification in the work they accomplish together and in helping the man she loves. However, a position as *assistant* to the man most important in one's life can be deadly to a woman's view of herself as fully mature, independent, and successful professionally.

You may recall the case of Marian, who was in love with her teacher, Harold. She was very tempted to become his assistant, and I urged her to think very carefully about the possible consequences of such a move that were certainly not part of her fantasies. She was already "in love" with him, and part of this compliant girl's way of loving was to give up her own needs and viewpoints in favor of his whenever there was a conflict between them. Working as Harold's assistant could only heighten her tendency to regard him with awe, for now he would be her boss in addition to being her lover, and she would be tempted constantly to shelve her own conceptions in favor of his. Her livelihood would also be dependent on Harold, and that, too, would provide a comfortable rationalization for her tendency to be a "good girl" and try to please him.

Obviously such an arrangement can bring out the most destructive aspects of a woman's submissiveness and can create a hothouse environment for her passivity and deference to men. Women must take responsibility for creating environments for themselves that will help them to achieve self-realization; they should not surround themselves with an environment that provides easy rationalizations for regression into childlike dependency or "feminine" deference to a male authority.

Some women solve a perceived conflict between equality and the possible loss of eroticism by choosing a field for achievement that requires entirely different skills than the lover's. If a woman has confidence that her skills and talents are valuable, she may "admire" her lover for exercising abilities for which she has no talent and still retain her self-esteem about her own skills. Or a woman may resolve this problem by attaching herself romantically to some authority in her own field who is so generally respected that she can feel he is the romantic, sexy "daddy" she "needs" but whose specific skills and interests are different enough from her own that she realizes she too can offer something intellectually valuable to their discussions.

Obviously both partners have a strongly vested interest (their eroticism) in this daddy-little girl situation. They need to learn how to relate erotically to each other without relying on the stereotyped behaviors of these roles. Therapy is usually necessary for both of them because of the extreme anxiety they may feel about the possible loss of their sexual love for each other without these behaviors. In reality, the excitement of relating to each other in new ways that no longer keep them distant from each other in a parent-child situation often contributes a great deal to their sexual fulfillment. A new kind of intimacy can be frightening to two people who have experienced each other as father and daughter, but with therapy to help them understand and deal with their anxieties they are likely to find much greater pleasure in each other.

3

Sex

The Elusive Orgasm

Ours is a highly competitive society, where great value is placed on achieving top scores on IQ and school tests, in sports events, and in amount of income earned (or married into, in the case of some women). The essence of competition is to show that one person is better than another; the winner is the one who scores higher than everyone else. It is not satisfying to the competitive person to be merely competent, even very competent, unless there is someone he or she can be better than. Even though a competitive person may understand intellectually that the need to "win" may well be destructive to his or her enjoyment of the activity itself, he or she nonetheless may constantly look for a competitor against whom to measure performance, for only through being better than someone else does the competitive person feel temporarily secure about her or his adequacy.

Although it is not considered polite for little girls to be outspoken about their desire to win, to be better than someone else, they learn from their parents and other socializing agents that the culture values success in competition for them just as it does for boys. In sexual concerns boys compete with each other with regard to penis size, to the number of girls and women "made" (this is even called "scoring"), and, as they grow toward middle age, with regard to the number of erections and orgasms achieved within a given time period. Men compete with themselves as well as with other men, measuring their later performance scores against those of their earlier years.

Until recently, girls competed sexually in ways that were less directly related to sexual *performance*, for it was considered shameful for a girl to admit that she had participated in sexual intercourse. Bragging that she slept with *x* number of boys would bring her not acclaim but disapproval. As a result girls adopted other ways of competing with each other sexually, depending on the social norm. For example, in the 1930s and 1940s it was important to be "popular," which meant having as many different "dates" as possible. In the 1950s it was important to "go steady" and to be "pinned" to one particular boy. It was always important to get engaged-to-be-married, for marriage was, and still is, the one sure mark of successful sexual "achievement" for a girl, particularly if the man who has chosen her, whom she has "won," has high status by reason of his family background or future professional prospects.

Whether or not women have orgasms during intercourse has recently become an important part of competitive sexual concerns. One unfortunate result of this new attitude is that many women are becoming just as anxious about how many and how powerful their orgasms are as men are about their erections and

ejaculations. Women are beginning to use "orgasm ef-
ficiency" as a measure of their sexual adequacy. In order
to estimate their "potency" many women now need to
measure their "performance" against that of other
women. For many women sexual activity is becoming
what it is for some, if not most, men: reassurance regarding their capacity for excellent performance. Instead of
enjoying a new way in which they can be like some men—
that is, feeling as free as men to engage in and enjoy sex
for its own sake without fear of social disapproval—many
women are copying the worst aspects of male sexuality,
placing the emphasis on "scoring" rather than on shared
fun and intimacy, and on the orgasms as *symbolic,* as
reassurance, rather than as one among many sources of
sexual pleasure.

SALLY: *"I'm jealous of Jean's ability to have multiple orgasms."*

Sally and her husband had been married for nine years
when they met another married couple who suggested
that they "swing" together. Never having done this
before, they thought it might be fun and interesting.
Neither of them bargained for what happened to Sally's
self-esteem. Her husband became involved with Jean,
the other woman, and he told Sally all about his sexual
delights with her. He reported to Sally (they felt an "open
marriage" required that they share everything) that Jean
was able to experience multiple orgasms regularly. In
contrast, Sally was not very orgasmic during intercourse;
she came maybe once every four or five times they made
love, and even then her orgasms seemed to her weak and
not satisfying.

Comparing her sexual response to Jean's, on the basis
of her husband's information, was especially painful to
Sally because she had grown up in the shadow of a twin
sister who was considered by their parents to be more

brilliant and more beautiful than she. Unfortunately Sally was unable as a youngster to express her jealousy and insecurity to anyone, for her parents had imposed upon her the role of the good, agreeable, self-sacrificing daughter and had allotted her sister the role of the temperamental, demanding, and uncooperative daughter. When she was a child and an adolescent Sally's self-esteem was built primarily on her image of herself as uncomplaining and pleasant, and indeed she strove to be "better" than her sister in these qualities.

It is easy to imagine how certain aspects of such an uncomfortable sibling experience could be repeated in the sexual arena in later life. Sally came to therapy as a very anxious young woman who still felt that she should be a "good sport." To her, this meant hiding her anxiety and fury in response to her husband's disconcerting and hostile gossip about his new lover's "perfect" sexual behavior. Feeling unable to compete with Jean in sexual performance (and therefore, she assumed, sexual desirability), as she had felt unable to compete with her sister's attractiveness and school performance, Sally trapped herself by relying all the more on the only "good" quality she felt she had in abundance: a willingness to swallow such "ugly" feelings as hurt and rage and to appear agreeable at any cost.

As a result of her family history Sally was highly sensitized to feelings of competition with and inferiority to another woman. She was liberated enough to have the expectation of achieving orgasms regularly during intercourse, but when she did not, she blamed her "inadequacy," a feeling that was intensified when her husband offered her data by which to compare herself unfavorably with another woman in his life.

Regardless of what attitude Sally might have toward her orgasms if she had more of them (perhaps she would see them as assurance of her ability to "succeed" in competition), she had a right to have them. I believe that her particular difficulty was related to two problems that many women experience as a result of their socialization as women in this culture. One stems from protecting their image as pure and spiritual, the other from suppressing anger.

If a woman learns that only the man's needs and timing count, or if she is too "well brought up" or ladylike to discuss her sex organs out loud for fear that such body references, and, indeed, the orgasm itself, might shock his sensibilities and send him careening out of bed, obviously the woman isn't going to have an orgasm. (But *he* will!)

Women who do have orgasms frequently are not in any way physically or psychologically "superior" to those who don't. They may, however, be more verbally "daring" and are probably less awed by the men they go to bed with. It's my belief that the reason some women have orgasms with lower-status lovers, à la Lady Chatterley, is that these lovers aren't the men these women have been taught to pamper and protect. They do not value the esteem of men who are younger, of a lower class, or in some other important way "inferior" to them, and so some women feel freer to communicate their sexuality to these lovers. If a woman sleeps with a man whom she sees as having significantly more prestige than she (and that may be any man of even her own social class), she may find it hard to reveal herself sexually. For thousands of years women have "serviced" men's sexual needs. If a woman is to have an orgasm she has to be able to view the man as available to "service" her. He probably is, but she may have to put herself on the line and display her body, her needs, and, God forbid, her excitement!

One more word about men's sensibilities: Lots of women, even the most beautiful, hate their own bodies. Our bodies are symbols of our social inferiority, and we often project onto them our self-denigration. Some of us don't like our noses or hair or plumpness, but very often it's some aspect of our sexual physique that is the vehicle for our projected self-hate. We are often embarrassed and ashamed of our tits, our asses, our cunts, and all the verbal and physical manifestations of our female sexuality such as moans and screams of delight during orgasm or the involuntary release of drops of urine and the odors of vaginal lubrication during sexual arousal. We may then incorrectly assume that men find our bodies as unappetizing as we do. The awful thing about this is that, in acting out the overprotective role most of us have learned in relation to male sensibilities, we try to hide these things from men's awareness. Men don't often worry about offending women with their sexual grunts, groans, or heavy breathing, or their wondrous, noisy peeing from the heights. How many men have you known who act embarrassed if a sound escapes their lips as they come? Contrast this with the way a woman feels if her vagina makes suction noises when the going (or coming) really gets good! She wants to hide under the bed or, worse yet, make it all go away! Too often she succeeds.

Women also don't like to offend men by asking them to fuck during a period, in case the man should grow faint at the sight (or, heaven help us, the taste) of blood, even though this can be one of the most sexually exciting times for women. Nor does a woman want to take too long in coming lest her lover get tired or bored with his "work." She, however, is supposed to be grateful for the opportunity to go on sucking or fucking forever to get him to come a second or third or fourth time. Oh, that I had a nickel (or better, an orgasm) for every woman who fears it takes her "too long" for even her first orgasm; better to fake it so he can go ahead and have his. Princes shouldn't have to wait, and aren't we taught that all men are princes compared to what *we* are without our clothes and party manners?

I want to emphasize that in *most* cases our assumption that men are disgusted by our bodies and our intimate functions is a projection of our own self-contempt and shame. In *most* cases men actually like fondling, licking, hearing, and smelling us or could learn to like these things if we could relax and let them.

I believe, however, that the major reason Sally did not have more orgasms was her suppression of her anger at her husband and her failure to recognize and deal with his anger. The fact that he told Sally about Jean's orgasms is evidence that he wanted to hurt her, for reasons that were never discussed between them because neither of them was willing to deal with his hostility. Sally had learned that nice little girls don't reveal their hurt and rage, especially when they feel themselves to be in the "wrong"—that is, "unsuccessful" in relation with another woman.

Sally suppressed the anxiety and anger she experienced at the hostile way her husband was using his affair, and by so doing she probably turned this anger against herself, perhaps in order to punish herself for not being the good sport she wished she could be. Like many women she sacrificed her own feelings in order not to "rain on his parade," with the result that she deprived herself of sexual pleasure and of a real encounter with *all* of her own and her husband's feelings, which might eventually have led to a better, more honest relationship between them. Therapists are familiar with the connection between sex and aggression. Neither men nor women can inhibit their angry feelings and still be free enough emotionally to experience great sex.

When Old Sexual Fantasies Fail the New Woman

BARBARA: *"My mind goes blank and I can't come."*

A few months ago, at a meeting of our feminist therapist group, one of the therapists presented the situation of her patient Barbara, who was no longer able to "turn on" during lovemaking. After hearing her story other women therapists who were present acknowledged that they had patients with the same problem, and some said that they themselves were experiencing a dilemma like Barbara's in their own sex lives.

Barbara is a young woman who, like many "normal" women, produced "masochistic" fantasies for herself during love play, which she found arousing. In most of these fantasies she portrayed herself as the unwilling victim of a man's sexual aggression. Sometimes she would imagine herself being tied to a mast and raped by a handsome, rough pirate. Sometimes she would be an old-fashioned, naive young servant sexually assaulted by the master of the house. Sometimes she would be attacked by a robber who intruded into her apartment. In all cases, it wasn't her "fault" that she "found" someone fucking her; he would "overcome" her (weak) resistance, and she'd be "just lying there," coming all over the place.

Recently, however, Barbara interpreted her therapist's exploration with her of her passivity and the ideals of the women's movement as meaning that it is "wrong" to be a passive victim. She was now finding that she felt too guilty about her eroticization of the victim's role to produce her old fantasies. As a result she was definitely less aroused than she had been. What was she to do?

(I described Barbara's dilemma to a male friend of mine who is also a therapist. "What can a woman do with a problem like this?" I asked him. He replied dryly, "I

guess she'll just have to relate to the person she's with."
Hmm.)

I don't usually believe that a therapist should meddle
too much with the nonrational elements in "instinctual"
activities. People certainly ought to be supported in whatever sources of pleasure they have, no matter how
ideologically impure, as long as they are not clearly
harmful to the self and others. It seems ridiculous to me
that people should have to feel guilty for their fantasies.
On the contrary, we should probably encourage people
to be *less* rational rather than more rational in sexual
encounters. Sex ought to be one of the places where we
can really act crazy and far-out with ourselves and with
our partners. That's one of the things intimacy is all
about—sharing thoughts and acts in private that you
can't parade before the outside world.

It appears to me that a therapist should encourage her
women patients when they want to give up a passive
life-style. However, if they want to hang on to the fantasy
of themselves as sexual victims, what's the harm, provided that the therapist can help them to distinguish
between playing the victim in sexual fantasy and acting
out the victim role in real life? When passive or aggressive sexual fantasies are acted out in the sexual situation, they can be playful. If a woman can clearly distinguish between play-acting and real life, there probably
will be no harm done. But, you may say, isn't this
argument support for "compartmentalization," and isn't
that "bad"? Aren't people supposed to be "integrated,"
and isn't that "good"? So, what else is new?

There is, however, an important feminist issue here
that must be explored with the patient. A woman's
tendency to portray herself as a passive victim in sexual
encounters derives from the culture's value that sexual
feelings are forbidden for girls. It is easy for young girls
to accommodate to this destructive attitude by imagining
themselves in sexual scenes where they are unwilling or

indeed unconscious (literally) participants. To imagine themselves as active and awake, much less as deliberately provoking or planning for a sexual encounter, would arouse so much anxiety that pleasurable sexual feelings could not arise. Someday, one hopes, all people will be able to free themselves of sexual repressions and stereotypes so that men as well as women will not feel stuck in any one role but can experience the pleasure of a variety of different psychological (as well as physical) postures.

Awakening Sexuality in the Older Woman

LENORE: *"My husband wants me to become a swinger."*

Lenore, a striking fifty-five-year-old executive, told me she had come to see me at the request of her husband, also aged fifty-five, who had announced that he wanted her to join him in "swinging." His request, clearly intended to help him alleviate the guilt he felt about *his* intentions, seemed to her "a stunning display of his insensitivity to where I'm at sexually," but she nevertheless agreed to see a therapist because she felt solely responsible for the lack of sexual activity between them. It had been many years since they had had any sexual relations at all. Lenore had imagined that her husband had a secret woman friend whose presumed existence she condoned, for she felt that so long as he had someone else he would not "bother" her about sex. When she realized that, on the contrary, he had been faithful all these years, was only now determined to emerge from their sexual desert, and even felt that he needed her cooperation to do so, she was both touched and frightened.

In her first consultation Lenore assured me that if it were entirely up to her, she would do absolutely nothing to change what she called her "lack of interest" in sex. She gave many "reasons" for her desire to remain as she was, which sounded superbly well considered: She was not attracted to her husband, who she assumed understood and accepted that fact, but who else, she reasoned, would be "available" to a fifty-five-year-old woman, much less interested in her; she was too old and too self-satisfied to undertake the process of psychotherapy; she was thoroughly involved in her career and felt no need to take up sex at this late date; she had lived "happily" this long without sex; she was perfectly comfortable with the image of herself as a woman who wasn't particularly interested in sex and didn't "need" sex in order to be happy; and so on. "After all," she declared, "why should everyone need sex? Aren't people different?"

In spite of her apparent confidence in her feelings about her asexual life, Lenore seemed to want assurance that she could do what she wanted with her sexuality, even ignore it, without feeling guilty or responsible to her husband. Although I was sorry that Lenore didn't want to experience sexual pleasure, I was not hopeful about her chances for change in this respect, for she seemed determined to stay where she was sexually. I did hope that she would recognize during that first consultation that her husband had changed and that her marriage was not going to remain as it had been for so many years, and, further, that she was indeed in control of her sexuality, and no one could take that control away from her. Lenore chose to deny the first reality and would not consider the possible consequences of her denial, which was her right. She felt relieved and content with the second. It was her contention that if she opened herself up sexually she would not be doing something for herself but for her husband.

It was not desirable in the course of that one session to try to convince her that she was denying herself something good in order to refuse him what he would also enjoy: her sexual love. It was obvious to me that Lenore's "asexuality" had to do with other problems these two were having, both as individuals and as a couple, and that she had chosen lack of interest in sex as a way of expressing these other tensions. I didn't know her well enough to identify these other tensions. Perhaps she was angry at her husband; perhaps she was afraid of close psychological contact; perhaps neither of them knew how to defend his or her boundaries in an intimate relationship; perhaps he helped her to feel undesirable; perhaps she felt controlled. Who could tell without knowing both of them better?

A month or so later Lenore called to say that she would like to start therapy with me, and that this time it would be for herself and not because her husband wanted her to change. Indeed, she had not told him of her plan to begin therapy. Eventually it became clear that Lenore really *was* interested in sex. One of her problems was that, like many women, she had never really believed that sexual responsiveness was something that could belong to a woman. It seemed to her that a woman's orgasm was something to be worn on a man's penis like a medal, something *he* achieved rather than a pleasure she had made possible for herself *with* him. Such phrases of her mother's as "Men only want to take advantage of you," "Men are only interested in one thing," and "Don't let him have his way with you" came up often in Lenore's therapy. They had convinced her that only men, not women, wanted sex and that sex was *all* men wanted in a relationship and all a woman *could* contribute to a relationship. No wonder Lenore preferred to pretend to herself and others that sex didn't exist for her and tried to show her dissatisfaction in the relationship with her husband by refusing to "give in" sexually.

As therapy progressed and Lenore expressed a desire

to explore her sexuality with a man, she and her husband joined a couples' group in addition to Lenore's continuing in individual therapy. (I feel that if a patient is a member of an intimate "system," such as a family or couple, the best therapy for her may include group sessions with as many members of that system as are willing to attend.) I did not suggest sex therapy at that time because it seemed to me that if Lenore's lack of attraction to her husband was due to unresolved tensions between them, these should be explored with him before they attempted sexual relations. I knew that such an exploration might, of course, help them decide to end the marriage and begin again with more promising partners if that's what they found they wanted to do.

Most people change a great deal in thirty years (the duration of this couple's marriage), and it is neither pathological nor unusual for people who have been married to each other that long to decide they want a change of partners. This is exactly what happened to Lenore and her husband. Lenore found an attractive young man who wanted to give her "sex therapy" himself, and this seemed to suit her very well. He was no gigolo who preyed on the frustrations of older women but was a self-sufficient businessman who had been married previously to a young woman who had died of leukemia. He relished the opportunity to introduce a beautiful and appreciative older woman to sexual pleasures he had once enjoyed and now missed. Like many other older women with younger lovers, Lenore and her man are a devoted couple. She no longer speaks of her "disinterest" in sex.

There are several feminist issues in Lenore's case. The most obvious is that her culture, transmitted through her mother, conned her into disowning her sexuality. To Lenore her sexuality seemed not to belong to her but to be entirely at the disposal of men, so she could readily imagine denying her sexual nature altogether rather than "give" it to a man with whom she was angry. Her action here was like that of some children whose parents interfere in their activities. These children often choose to do nothing with their abilities rather than "give" their achievements to their parents. Their view (learned from their parents' possessive attitudes) is that it is their parents, not themselves, who "own" their efforts.

Very often in a marriage each partner assumes that the sexual behavior of the other belongs to him or her, although this is probably more often the case with husbands. In many countries, husbands still have the legal right to their wives' sexual "services," whereas the wives do not legally have or feel that they have the same rights regarding their husbands' sexual attentions. Many, many men even in our own culture see intercourse with their wives as their right, and too often the wives concur that this is, indeed, their conjugal "obligation." What is construed as a duty rarely becomes a pleasure. Most people would rather withdraw from a required activity than engage in it without experiencing freedom of choice.

Another feminist issue in Lenore's situation was the ease with which she was able to assume that she could be simply "disinterested" in sex without considering this a pathological condition. Few if any men would do that. If a man felt himself not interested in sex he would run like hell to the nearest doctor for something: an operation, an aphrodisiac, advice, even psychotherapy. Many women, however, particularly older women like Lenore, assume that their lack of interest in sex is probably normal. If an older woman *does* experience her sexual apathy as a problem, she may be very reluctant to expose her interest in changing it to a physician or psychotherapist. Even many younger women hesitate to reveal to doctors (male authority-figures) their eagerness to become more sexually responsive, so great are the cultural barriers in many communities against a woman's viewing sexual fulfillment as her natural prerogative.

Whenever I have described this case, the response has been that the denouement recounted above must be fantasy: People are so accustomed to predicting only a sexual wasteland for the older woman who has left her husband or is widowed, or who has heretofore chosen (consciously or unconsciously) to be unattached. This again is a bias against seeing the older woman alone as sexual and happy! We imagine that widows must weep forever, that women in their sixties and seventies must be content with each other or their children and grandchildren. Not at all! There is nothing wrong with a woman's happily choosing to remain sexually and emotionally uninvolved with men, and indeed I hope that the women's movement will make this a respectable choice for more women. However, if a woman who is middle-aged or older *wants* to be sexually and romantically active and if she is willing to stretch her previous definition of who is acceptable as a lover, she may have surprisingly little difficulty in finding a devoted sexual partner! She needs the courage and self-esteem to be able to perceive herself as deserving of this kind of excitement and fulfillment, however, and she needs to be able to exercise an aggressiveness that may at first be awkward for her. Most people, including prospective lovers, will still expect her to stay in the corner and suffer. More about this in the chapter on loneliness. Here's to fucking forever!

4

Work

Passivity

PEGGY: *"It seems as if I'm always starting all over again."*

Peggy came to New York from an exciting two-year stint as a Peace Corps volunteer. She expected that the same sense of direction and involvement would continue to characterize her life in the city. She found, however, that without a close-knit group of supportive colleagues and a clear-cut, short-term work goal defined for her by an outside source, such as the Peace Corps provided, she became bored and uninvolved. She entered therapy because she felt "flat" emotionally and because in two critical areas, her work life and her love life, she did not feel that she was working toward anything fulfilling. Her subjective experience was that nothing was happening and that she did not know how to make anything happen. Nor was she at all sure of what she wanted to happen.

Peggy chose to settle in New York after her service in the Peace Corps because she wanted to be near Ron, a childhood sweetheart with whom she still had a vague off-again, on-again relationship. Ron attended graduate school in New York, but Peggy had no plans for herself other than to see if their relationship would develop into something more defined. While she was waiting, Peggy taught school, without any particular interest or involvement, and indeed, with a new anxiety: She was beginning to realize that teaching was not really for her. She didn't like being the center of the students' attention; she felt uncomfortable in the role of an authority figure and overwhelmed by a group of children, although she could enjoy relating to them individually. She decided not to teach again the following fall.

Occasionally Peggy would say that she didn't know what she was doing in New York. She had been in the city for six years but had not really tried to find a niche for herself. Every fall she got some kind of job, which she dropped in June in order to spend the summer with her family or to travel with a girlfriend. When she came back, to be near Ron (whom she saw infrequently), she had to start over in some other job. Gradually it dawned on Peggy that she could not find an identity through Ron. He was apparently content with their tenuous attachment and not interested in giving her a role to enact in relation to him. She appeared to be stuck with her pattern of starting all over each fall in some kind of work that interested her very little, paid poorly, and provided no challenge to her intelligence.

Peggy's therapy chiefly involved working on her passivity, which in her case was an expression of hostility toward her parents, particularly toward her mother, who always overinvolved herself in Peggy's enterprises. Like many women, Peggy had learned to be "ladylike." She had been forbidden as a child to express anger openly toward her parents or to criticize them. At any rate she was conned out of her anger by frequent reminders from each parent that the other was a model of parental generosity and rectitude. After all, was not her father a respected professional and her mother a darling to be so interested in Peggy's work and achievements?

The truth was that Peggy experienced her mother's intrusions into her projects as a pain but was never able to say so. When she finally recognized that her mother's overinterest meant not only love for her but hostile interference and distrust of Peggy's abilities and identity as a separate person she was able to express her passionate resentment of this interference.

Passivity is a socially approved behavior for women. Very few people would even notice that Peggy was doing anything different from the norm. Because her anger so often cannot be expressed directly, the angry young woman may fall into a kind of stupor, supported by the culture. As she separated herself from her angry (though repressed) involvement with her mother, Peggy began to feel more lively and to care more about doing good things for herself.

Except for her extreme passivity, Peggy's lack of motivation for sustained work outside the home is the rule and not the exception for women in our culture. Many grown women are stuck with the lack of psychological preparation for self-support that we give to men. In the long psychological preparation for assuming the role of primary wage-earner, most men develop an identity organized around work competency. They take this identity seriously and for the most part do not have the "temporary" feeling about work that many women have. This view of work as temporary or as only play often prevents women from achieving a feeling of "getting someplace"—that is, building up for themselves a progressive sense of accomplishment, financial security, and real competency. After twenty years or so in a profession, most men can feel that they are skilled, and they know who they are at least in a work sense. This can be a significant aspect of anyone's self-esteem.

I am certainly not suggesting that men's typically serious, nonplayful attitude toward their work is all good. As a matter of fact, if people take their work too seriously we detect in them a joylessness and an obsessive quality that may hinder the development of other parts of their personalities, but I have very little doubt that by and large men's work orientation gives them much more than women's lack of work commitment gives them. The most important advantage, among many, of having a serious work commitment is that it gives people choices. A woman who can do nothing but housekeep and who suddenly or by choice finds herself without a particular man must either find another man, if she can, among some specimens who may not be particularly desirable to her or live at the poverty level. Further, when women are not prepared psychologically to work, to say nothing of not being prepared educationally, they often feel victimized and furious at their bad luck or at the injustice of life, which "forces" them to seek employment. Men as a rule are spared these energy-sapping feelings. They may sometimes regard work as burdensome, but only the most passive-dependent men feel outraged by the need to work.

We need to provide women with the same expectations and the same opportunities for a satisfying and financially remunerative work life as we give to men. Having few avenues for meaningful self-expression and feelings of insecurity about being able to care for themselves now and in the future, young women such as Peggy are likely to develop painful psychological problems such as depression and feelings of identity confusion that their fantasy can be resolved only by attaching themselves to a man.

Sometimes even women who have been well prepared for a career or profession and who are very successful at it experience serious role conflicts that inhibit their enjoyment and occasionally paralyze the enaction of one of their valued roles. This was exactly the problem that Connie brought to psychotherapy.

Role Conflicts

CONNIE: *"I feel too anxious away from my daughter to go to the office."*

Connie was the mother of a "terrible two," tyrannical, temperamental, and egocentric (like most healthy two-year-olds). She was feeling pushed around by her daughter and constrained from disciplining her by her belief that a "good" mother doesn't impose her needs on her child. Although Connie was a successful architect, she had some old-fashioned values with regard to the role of motherhood. These values, which were more appropriate to her mother than to her, made her feel guilty about working and "abandoning" her little girl. Connie found herself having anxiety attacks when she went back to work after her daughter's birth.

Connie came to a feminist therapist because intellectually she believed that she ought to be able to combine the roles of mother and professional woman, but her guilt and intense anxiety over being separated from her daughter made work away from home impossible. She was also unable to separate herself from her daughter to go on trips with her husband, and this was causing additional conflict between Connie and Greg, who felt that she was overprotecting their child. On the other hand, he himself made demands on her that indicated his own ambivalence toward her independence. For example, he would promise to do certain household chores but would find ways to renege on his promise. He would also ask for a good deal of mothering from Connie whenever he felt ill or psychologically uncomfortable. He was in the midst of a new enterprise in his own work at the same time Connie started therapy, and it seemed to him that he was entitled to her nurturing compassion for all the frustrations he had to endure in his project. In addition, he believed that his work demands precluded more than token child care on his part.

Unfortunately, this left Connie in a bind, because she was "afraid" to leave her little girl with a baby-sitter. These fears were aroused more by her own panic at being away from the child and by her suppressed rage toward her daughter and husband than by any real possibility of harm. So when Connie came to therapy she was feeling very inadequate as a mother, afraid of the anger and disapproval of her daughter, her husband, and her own mother. She was in intense psychological discomfort, feeling guilty much of the time for wanting to be free to work and yet in considerable pain because her "incapacitating" anxiety was making work impossible for her.

It was helpful to Connie, I believe, to see a woman therapist who also had a young child and who nevertheless often worked outside her home. Fortunately for me as a feminist as well as a mother, neither of my children seems to have turned out to be any more freakishly neurotic, scholastically retarded, or criminally inclined than children of mothers who don't work. One can, of course, go beyond personal experience to the psychological literature and find in the most impartial studies further evidence to prove what common sense suggests: that the children of mothers who like their work are no more or less crazy than the children of mothers who don't work at all outside the home. In most cases, kids are proud of and able and willing to adjust to their mothers' work commitments.

When Connie saw that it wasn't a God-given part of her femaleness that she be her husband's mother or her child's child she began to express her anger at both of them directly, in words, rather than by "lying down on the job" (hers). No longer consumed by guilt for not wanting to be a full-time mother to her daughter, she no longer had to punish herself by imagining that terrible things would happen to both of them if someone else shared the child's care. After a few months of therapy Connie went comfortably back to work, and the "terrible two" became a nicer child when she could no longer get a rise out of her mother by her manipulative antics. Now, several years later, Connie and her husband are expecting another child, and Connie is looking forward without anxiety to having a full-time live-in housekeeper so that she will not have to stop working at all. If she does what she *wants* to do and feels sure that her children are being adequately cared for, there is no rule that says she *must* stay home for their "benefit." Nobody benefits from a mother's resentment, guilt, frustration, or anxiety attacks.

Fear of Self-Assertion on the Job

CARLA: *"I'm afraid of these 'grown-ups' and can't ask for anything."*

One of the most common work-related difficulties of women has to do with their inability to see themselves in high-paying jobs, in positions of authority and influence over others, and their inhibitions about asking for more money and power once they are in a job. Certainly it is true, and I don't wish to minimize it, that women are held back from good jobs by discrimination against them when they seek admittance to graduate schools or to prestigious business or professional firms and from high pay by discrimination on the job. But this problem is exacerbated by the fact that girls are taught it isn't nice to be aggressive. It is all the more important and therefore all the more difficult for some women to assert themselves in the face of probable rejection and discouragement from the very people whose support they need.

Carla came to New York from Venezuela to work as a free-lance reporter representing whatever South American television networks would give her assignments on topics of interest to their audiences. A skilled reporter, she had nevertheless found it hard to make a living in Venezuela, where there is even more discrimination against women in the media than in the United States.

Every few months Carla had to go back to South America to gather assignments for the next period of work, and it was always agonizing for her to face the rebuffs she frequently encountered from station managers and news executives. The problem she brought to therapy was that she found it difficult to ask for a good salary and for an adequate expense account. She felt she should be very grateful for any crumb she got. Gradually she began to see that she was, after all, providing the networks that contracted for her services with excellent work in a highly competitive market. Through therapy she worked through much of her lifelong fear of male "authorities." She was also able to recognize how angry (and provocative) she often was toward the men whose assignments she fulfilled and how difficult it was for her to see herself as their equal. Instead of being able to cooperate with them as professional to professional, she accepted their view of her as a rebellious, if talented, little girl, so she asked for less than she deserved. She got back at them for giving her less and for making teasing fun of her by being late with assignments, by picking little fights with these men, and by being reluctant to do assignments on the subjects the television stations were interested in. When she finally saw herself as a skilled professional, as skilled as the men with whom she worked, she demanded more respect for herself, and she got it. She also stopped picking fights and messing around with the assignments. In a very short time she felt confident enough to apply for and accept a job as head of the New York office of one of South America's most prestigious magazines.

In some ways Carla's radical political values are at variance with those of the magazine for which she now works. I bring this up because one of the common criticisms of psychotherapy is that it helps people to adjust to a conventional "norm" and does not encourage them to support social change. What psychotherapy can and frequently does do is help people to reach the point of personal freedom where they can choose to do what they want. Carla had to compromise some of her political beliefs to work with Venezuelan television anyway, but even so she found that she could make some cogent personal statements about politics once she felt less afraid of her bosses. This is exactly what happened in her new job, too. She was making a very substantial political statement just by being a woman of status in this kind of organization. In addition, she, a woman, was respected and recognized as a reporter of great skill and sensitivity. Carla is now an employer of women herself and a person who has considerable influence over the news stories that are printed concerning American affairs. Because she is genuinely skilled and respected, her stories, even the many she chooses to write about social change or radical politics, are respected also, and she reaches many more people than when she was putting together shows on her own.

5

Motherhood

The Potential Mother

JOANNE: *"I've been thinking of having a baby on my own."*

Joanne was a twice-divorced college teacher in her late thirties. Full of enthusiasm and energy, she was a very attractive and persuasive woman. It seemed that her previous husbands, as she described them in therapy, were men with considerable personality problems of which Joanne had been aware but, in her eagerness to marry, had rationalized away. She suspected, she said, that marriage to either of these men might be a touch-and-go proposition, but she "found" herself ignoring her doubts and proceeding (as she realized later) chiefly on the basis of her hopes and wishes.

Joanne began therapy because she was having a hard time making a decision about having a child. This was

67

one of the two things she very much wanted; the other was success in her career. However, she had not completed any research projects, and publication was an explicit requirement for advancement in her field. Since she was not involved with a man, Joanne was considering whether she could bring up a child on her own and still achieve the professional recognition that she also desired.

As her therapy progressed it seemed clear to both of us that in characteristic fashion Joanne was blinding herself to some of the realities of child care and motherhood. She discovered that it was the idea of having a child and being a mother that turned her on, just as she liked the idea of being a recognized professional in her field better than actually doing the research and writing that would make success a reality. Like so many women, Joanne had learned that approval and prestige accrue to women in our culture who are mothers, and so she came to see motherhood as a desirable goal.

To handle success in both motherhood and a profession at the same time, a woman in our culture has to be alert to the realistic demands of each enterprise and very skilled in allocating her attention and energy. Joanne, however, seemed to operate mostly on the basis of fantasy. For example, she had never spent much time alone with a child, so she had no real experience by which to assess the demands and needs of a child. Nor had it occurred to her that she might experience great resentment toward a child if she had one exactly at the time when she must dig into research and publication in order to achieve the academic recognition that she also coveted.

Joanne decided that she could get to know children better if she did her research with children in the public schools. She found that she enjoyed this so much that it helped her make her decision in an entirely unexpected way. She felt that she could continue this kind of involvement with children and by so doing satisfy her need to be near children without being as responsible for them as she would as a mother.

The women's movement has made it possible for women like Joanne, married or unmarried, to make the decision not to have children without feeling unduly deprived or inadequate as women. But it is much less supportive of women who are already mothers or who want to become mothers. In fact, many feminists today are arguing that motherhood is the role that is most destructive to women, and one can detect in much feminist literature other attitudes of denigration toward childrearing. This point of view is turning mothers off from the movement. What they want is not to be insulted by their sisters but to be supported by them, not to be told that somehow they are disloyal fools for choosing to have children and to rear them but to be helped to be more comfortable and self-respecting in their role as mothers as they are helped to be more comfortable and self-respecting in their nondomestic roles. I would like to see the women's movement provide support groups specifically for mothers to help them use their new self-respect in asking for more for themselves from their families and from their society, such as low-cost children's centers and more tax benefits for working mothers.

As a therapist who is also a mother I'm aware that my work with patients who are mothers or who are deciding whether or not to have children is necessarily influenced by my own experiences. Motherhood was and still is tremendously gratifying to me, and I will undoubtedly feel a great loss when my younger child leaves the house for good. I know myself well enough to anticipate that no matter how liberated I may be from the culture's pressure to have children or how effectively my profession provides me with personal involvement of a different kind, I will be depressed and probably somewhat anxious when I no longer have a young child at home to care for or a medium-sized one with whom to share the excitement of new intellectual interests and growing interpersonal awareness. Even now, I daydream from time to time about having a grandchild and congratulate myself on my cleverness at having produced children who are sixteen years apart so that my son is already married while my daughter is still a little girl. I am obviously about to become one of those mothers who pesters her married children about *when* "it" is going to happen! But that's okay. I'm not ashamed of my anticipation, and if they don't like it, they'll find ways to handle me.

Clearly the feminist issue in Joanne's case is that a woman no longer need be dependent for self-esteem and social approval on her role as a mother. An important problem about making the decision not to become a mother, however, is that it will be irrevocable at precisely the time of life when a woman might want to have the solace and warmth that grown or almost grown children can provide. (At least one child usually turns out to like his or her mother!) One hears many childless women say that they wish they had had children; one hardly ever hears a mother who has grown children say that she is sorry she had children, except in a mood of irritability or depression that may not be really related to her children or to motherhood. (Children are, after all, easy to use as scapegoats for our other problems; they are right there, causing *some* trouble, all the time.)

It is well and good for the women's movement to support those women who do not want to have children or who for one reason or another associate motherhood with unbearable self-sacrifice and drudgery. On the other hand, it is surely a therapeutic issue to explore with such women the possible consequences of their decision as well as the psychological characteristics that may be contributing to it, such as an intolerance for intimacy or a tendency to sacrifice future goals for present comfort or a feeling of rivalry with a newcomer. To deal only with the feminist issue may deprive a woman of information about herself that may be important in making a decision satisfactory to her not only now but in her future as well.

The Dominated Mother

A clear feminist issue is raised for many mothers when they have a domineering child. In my opinion the child has generally learned this behavior toward his or her mother from some other member of the family or even from the submissiveness of the mother herself. Most frequently the model is—guess who?—the father. He may not be the only model for the child's derogatory attitudes and behavior toward mom, however. There are at least two other prime suspects: the mother's parents, particularly her mother, and the child's older siblings.

The key point is that usually someone of importance to the child is patterning the child's behavior toward the mother. The first step in dealing with this problem, therefore, is a very practical and not "deep" analytic examination of the child's world of human influences. Somebody in this world is demonstrating that it's okay to debase women. When this person is found, it is necessary for the mother to confront the offender with the assertion that her child is learning, through the natural and healthy need to be like the older people he or she admires, an attitude that is personally hurtful to the mother and potentially harmful to the child's opinion of and relations with other women in the future. If the child is a girl, she is being seriously hampered in her ability to respect herself, today and in the future, since she is learning to be a woman like the mother she and others in the family now push around.

Let's look for a moment at the important older figures and the mother's interaction with them. The father's attitude may be something like the culturally convention-al one for men. He is the boss; he knows best regarding everyone's interest; he makes the decisions, and when he addresses his wife it is more often than not in a tone of scorn. On some level the mother agrees with him that women are supposed to be bossed around because they don't know what's best for themselves. And if *they* don't know what's best for themselves, how can they be sure they know what's best for their families, even for the youngest members? This is the hook upon which the mother abandons her self-possession as a reasonably au-thoritative parent whose suggestions and other remarks deserve respectful consideration. The children manage, like their father, to convince her that she can't know anything worthwhile, and consequently that their opin-ions and desires should be catered to. After all, isn't that what women are supposed to do, and isn't that what they do best—make other people happy by catering to them and respecting their wills and opinions more than their own?

It is especially painful to the mother (and children) when it is *her* mother who is the model for the children's dominating, disrespectful attitude; even more, perhaps, where the grandmother is still vigorous and competent around the household. I saw some of this (and still see it) very vividly in the interaction between my grandmother, an extraordinarily unpleasant and tyrannical woman, and my mother. My grandmother's vitriolic, abusive manner toward my mother still intimidates her, although my grandmother is in her mid-nineties and my mother is seventy. When my grandmother came to visit, my brothers and I couldn't help but notice how my mother, intellectually independent, usually aggressive, and very domineering herself (after all, her mother was her model), would shrink into some childlike, tentative posture before her own mother. These were the times when we children could also push her around.

A feminist therapist would help the dominated mother develop confidence first of all in her right to express her authority in her household and even more important in her right to have needs of her own. Certainly among the most important of these needs is the right to be respected as an important person in the family, not to be regarded and treated as the children's or father's subordinate, ready to do their bidding. Because so many women derive their self-esteem primarily from the feeling that they are desperately needed by other family members as indispensable adjuncts to a comfortable household, it is not easy in therapy to help them assert themselves in the face of their families' demands. I think it must be very difficult for most male therapists to understand the persistence with which many mothers allow their families to walk all over them. The concept of service to others is in no way a part of most men's ego-ideals as it is of most women's. It is very sad indeed to see women who are depressed or physically ill because of the really cruel demands made on them by their families and sadder to recognize how tenaciously some of these women resist a change in their roles. If they could not see themselves as willing servants they either would feel unbearably guilty or would expect to be imminently abandoned or abused verbally or physically.

I believe that it can be very useful for a mother who cannot assert herself or protect herself from exploitation by family members to be in treatment with a female (preferably feminist) therapist, who may be a model for what the patient needed but failed to see in her own mother. A woman therapist sensitive to the particular needs of such a patient should be able to provide her with support and encouragement for self-assertion and yet understand her guilt and her fear of alienating her family. Such a mother could also benefit from a woman therapist who herself was assertive in protecting her own interests yet who was not hostilely aggressive. (So many women fear that making demands of others and being confidently self-protective when others make demands of them means that they will be acting like "castrating" bullies—like the very worst models in their own lives!)

It should go without saying that a female therapist need not be a mother herself to respect and support women who are mothers, and that a mother who is looking for a female therapist need not restrict herself to therapists who have children. (As Margaret Mead retorted when asked if white, middle-class anthropologists could "really" understand primitive cultures, "You don't have to have been a horse to be a good veterinarian!") If a "dominated mother" in her therapy experiences reinforcement for her authority as a mother while at the same time recognizing that her children's needs must be considered realistically, if she notices that as a result of her therapy her children are beginning to respect her and like her and that she feels free to ask them for their cooperation without guilt and without pleading, if she learns how to ask for her mother's and husband's support for her needs and rights, then her therapy is being helpful to her as a woman who is also a mother, no matter who her therapist is.

The Overidentifying Mother

HELENE: *"My daughter never wants me around anymore."*

Helene came into therapy because of the tensions between her and her sixteen-year-old daughter, Jan. Jan complained that she needed more privacy and that she experienced her mother's avid interest in her dates, her record collection, her figure, her friendships with other girls, and her wardrobe as painfully intrusive. She was telling her mother more often and more directly to mind her own business. To Helene this seemed like rejection, and she became increasingly depressed and anxious.

I was shocked when I first saw Helene because I knew from the colleague who referred her that she was in her early forties, yet she was dressed like a teen-ager in knee-socks, loafers, sweater, and plaid kilt. She did not look depressed. On the contrary, her expression was bright and cheerful, her movements quick and perky. She spoke with a great deal of animation and gaiety, like a young girl just returning from an exciting event. (Needless to say, most people feel cautious and somewhat restrained by anxiety on their first visit to a therapist. When they speak it is often with hesitation and discomfort.)

As her therapy progressed it became clear that to Helene her own adolescence was the most interesting and energizing time in her life. Gradually she made contact with the emptiness and despair that she was experiencing in her present life except for those times when she could obliterate the boundaries between herself and her daughter and borrow Jan's appearance, life-style, personal tastes, and friends.

An important aspect of Helen's therapy was the work we undertook together on her relationship with her husband, whom she saw at the start of treatment as boring and ordinary. She was so focused on herself-as-adolescent and on her daughter's world that she scarcely knew who her husband was (much less who *she* was!) It was actually difficult for her to give a physical description of her husband. For many weeks, whenever she spoke of him, she referred to him as "my husband" rather than by name. He appeared dull to her because she was unwilling to look at him. When she began to recognize that she wanted him in her grown-up world, she noticed many interesting and attractive characteristics in him that she had not previously seen.

Helene was one of the many women who have been victimized by the media's myth that the only valuable females besides mothers are swinging teen-agers. When her daughter grew out of childhood into an exceptionally independent adolescence Helene could no longer derive self-esteem from her role as a mother. She turned back the clock of her psyche to her own adolescence and tried to cope with her imagined loss of social prestige and usefulness as a mother by identifying with her earlier self, presumably a cheerful and vibrant girl. Helene claimed that her adolescence had been a happy time for her. As evidence she pointed to her memories of her energy and excitement, which appeared to be in such contrast to the depression she was now experiencing underneath her teen-age identity. My own feeling is that she was a depressed adolescent, too, and that she reacted to her depression by denying it and assuming exactly the opposite state. At any rate, the "character" she assumed both in her remembered adolescence and in her middle-aged revival of it conformed to a cultural stereotype for young females: look good, be cheerful so that you'll be popular, and don't be serious about anything. Many young girls who are anxious and depressed prevent themselves from getting the help they need by presenting a façade of well-being and joyfulness. This is the image that's projected to them by teen-age fashion magazines and other media. Our culture expects girls and young women to be attractive and pleasant consorts for men no matter what their real feelings may be.

The Angry Mother

Although feelings of anger and frustration directed toward our children are as normal as anger toward anyone else with whom we share intimate daily contact, there are clearly some mothers who find themselves either chronically angry or extremely worried about their negative responses to their children. Some do not let themselves be aware of ever *feeling* angry at their children. Others who feel anger cannot let themselves *act* angrily toward the children. Such women may be diverting their angry feelings or behavior to such distractions as overeating or drinking, or they may be experiencing some of the physical symptoms that are associated with suppressed anger at "entrapment," such as skin disorders ("breaking out"), colitis (the "runs"), and migraines ("in a bind").

The feeling of being trapped (which increases anxiety and therefore aggressive feelings against the person or situation we experience as trapping us) often arises in mothers. Most women have grown up with the ideal of marrying and having children. After a woman fulfills that ideal she may realize that she doesn't like kids or child care. Perhaps she likes some children but dislikes her own, because the child really is unpleasant to be around or reminds her of someone she disliked intensely or had problems with in the past, such as a younger sibling or a childhood friend.

Being a mother sounded like a great idea as she was growing up, but she was never told that the reality of motherhood for a particular woman might stink. All of our young lives are directed toward this one primary goal—finally getting to be a mother. Nobody ever tells us what a chance we may be taking by putting all our eggs (so to speak) into this one basket, whose contents are not going to be revealed until it's psychologically very late to change our ideas of who we want to be and what else we might want to spend our energy and time doing. When I think of all the different personalities, talents, and yearnings that mothers may have and then think of all the different personalities that kids may develop, it seems totally absurd that we are taught from our own infancies that no matter who *we* are and no matter who *they* are, we're going to love our children and love caring for them!

Some women are able to say, "Okay, I don't like this scene or this kid, so I'm going to make the best of a bad thing by getting myself a good job that will take me out of the house during the day and a good housekeeper who does like taking care of children, and then nobody will suffer unduly from this unfortunate turn of events." Well, these are not usually the mothers who come to psychotherapy.

Most people feel at least temporarily helpless when they discover that something they've looked forward to for a lifetime isn't turning out as they expected, and they may turn this helpless feeling into rage at "fate" or at their specific circumstances. Women who feel trapped into motherhood and who feel guilty about wanting to get out may direct their distress at their children.

Most feelings of anger at children, however, are not the result of disliking children or motherhood. If you are a mother, you will probably find, when you stop to think about it, that there are very specific kinds of interactions with your child that are hard for you to manage, or that there are specific characteristics of the child, physical or psychological, that annoy you. Once it's possible to pinpoint these sore spots, mothers feel less overwhelmed by feelings of inadequacy and can go to work on the sources of frustration. They become problems to be solved, and there is indeed a way to relieve, if not to solve, most human problems. Nothing is perfect, but very little in human life is hopeless, even getting along with one's children. Trouble comes when people can't see any *specific* problem because they are fogged in by anxiety and therefore can't figure out a solution, or when they see a solution but don't (or won't) work toward it because they are too angry or because they feel helpless. For women who are not educated to do interesting, respected, well-paid work, the choices of what to do besides caring for children may be limited or unattractive to them, and their resentment is natural. The response to this painful problem does not have to be helpless rage turned against the child. A mother who feels this way will have to direct her energy toward effecting some change in her situation, no matter how infinitesimal or unappealing that change might appear at first. For some women the answer might be to join political or organizational efforts to help all women with this kind of problem; for some women the solution might be a few hours' work each week outside the house; for some women it might mean a more detailed examination of how they learned passivity and feelings of impotence from their upbringing and how they can change these feelings.

A mother may wish to learn more about children in the company of other mothers who have similar needs, so that she won't feel so isolated with her uncomfortable feelings and so that she can become more adept at the very real skills and techniques (not the *mystique*) of motherhood. She may find that she likes being a mother once she knows how, or she may find that the more she knows about it the *less* she likes it.

Recently, considerable attention has been given by the media to mothers who have decided to leave their husbands and children because they felt that their own growth required this action. As a feminist (and a mother) I can perceive the possible gains to everyone of such a decision if the mother is deeply convinced that there is no other acceptable way for her to realize herself. But as a therapist I know that such decisions can often be impulses acted upon in the belief that such action will solve all the tensions the person is experiencing. Very often, however, the problem comes from some other source, and leaving home not only does not solve the real problem but may add to the woman's distress.

Because a woman's decision to leave her family deeply affects the feelings and future of everyone in the family, it seems to me that the only responsible and reasonable course is for her to involve the whole family in her decision to leave, if possible. I do not believe she can bypass the opinions of other family members without experiencing guilt and isolation. These days the best setting for the exploration and involvement of everyone's feelings is family therapy.

Involving everyone in this way may dramatically change the old "gestalt" or structure of emotions and behavior among family members. New solutions may become evident that were not perceived before. Even if the mother holds to her decision to go, she will know how everyone feels, whom she can count on for support, whose anger she must yet deal with, and many other things that will be important to her in her new adjustment. Most crucially, she will know that she gave everyone a chance to be available to her and herself a chance to be available to them. This will help her feel good about herself no matter what her final decision.

The Lesbian Mother

In some sophisticated communities an increasing number of children are being adopted by homosexual parents and an increasing number of lesbians are choosing to give birth to babies. The reasoning of the adoption agencies is that a child is better off with a parent or parents who love him or her, regardless of the parents' sexual orientation, than in a series of foster homes. Most of the students in my child development classes, particularly those who have already raised a family, claim that they are distressed by the idea of the absence of a father figure in the home of a lesbian mother. They say, "Doesn't a child need both a mother and a father?" Well, I don't think that's what they are really worried about. I think the psychiatric establishment has done great harm to homosexuals in the past by labeling them as "sick." Although the American Psychiatric Association has now officially changed its diagnostic assessment of homosexuality to a "disturbance in sexual orientation," the idea persists that something is wrong with the gay person; his or her whole personality may no longer be officially labeled "disturbed," but his or her "sexual orientation" decidedly still is.

Does a child "need" both a mother and a father? I think that question is in the same category as "Does a child need good parents?" Sure, it would be nice if all children were reared by mothers *and* fathers, particularly by parents who are "good" to them, but to make this a part of the "rules" for raising happy children requires that we define what we mean by *nice* and what we mean by *good*. We would have to know exactly what functions or characteristics of the child are affected by not having parents who act this way, specifically, or that way, specifically. There is no evidence to suggest that a child who is reared by one parent is necessarily less advantaged than a child who is reared by two. And even if there were, we certainly don't know how such a child is disadvantaged. There seem to be other aspects of home life that are more important to the child's development than whether there are opposite-sexed parents: for example, whether the child lives in an atmosphere of love and acceptance most of the time, whether the parents' expectations that the child will do well in school and in life are reasonable and consistent, whether the parents participate in the child's learning from an early age, give adequate attention to his or her medical and nutritional needs, and so on.

The lesbian mother is not necessarily a "single" mother, since she may live with her lover, but the image of her as single reinforces the outsider's negative judgment of her because of her homosexuality. Derogatory attitudes toward the "single woman" as unwanted or ugly, sexually repressed or promiscuous, add to our distorted and prejudiced views of the homosexual woman as lascivious, shallow, and unstable. We use the term *deviate* to describe not only homosexuals but all sorts of sociopaths—those who expose themselves to little girls or fuck sheep or call up strangers to say dirty words to them. The lesbian mother has to cope with the stigma of her imputed singleness and all that goes with that and the stigma of her imputed "abnormality," plus the general public's notion of her as selfish and inconsiderate, if not irresponsible or even somewhat criminal, for "exposing" a child to her "emotional" disorders and "obscene" sexuality.

The reality may be very different from this grossly unfair image. For example, the lesbian mothers I have known are all living in relationships as stable (or unstable!) as any heterosexual one. In any case I don't feel that children need to be overprotected from the realities and varieties of human relationships and personalities. A child can adjust to the fact that he or she has a lesbian mother (or lesbian "parents"), as children always adjust to the fact that their parents may be atypical in one way or another. Some are fatter than most people in the neighborhood; some are richer; some are poorer; in some families the mothers are doctors or lawyers or school principals; in some families one or both parents are physically handicapped. Some parents are much older than the average; some are much younger. It seems to me ludicrous to suggest that an atypical family should not have a child (as long as the parents are mentally and physically capable of responding to the child's needs for care and attention) lest the child learn his parents' "abnormality" or feel unduly stigmatized by the parents' stigma. Even if these things occur, and there is no certainty that they will, they aren't fatal. Those of us who grew up with parents who were "different" suffered pain for that, but we also had an opportunity to look at things in ways that were different from conventional frames of reference. There's nothing wrong with having a family that's different if the parents can help the child to see that "different" is neither better nor worse than ordinary. It is also important for parents in such "different" families to resist the child's tendency to blame his or her problems on the family's obvious departures from a neighborhood "norm." Family differentness is a handy scapegoat for everybody's problems, and the "different" parent, particularly the mother, may be too ready to blame herself for tensions in family members that may have absolutely nothing to do with her unconventionality or atypicality.

6

Loneliness

SANDRA: *"I miss him so much when we aren't together that I'm afraid I'll have to find someone else who can be around more often."*

Sandra, a magazine editor in her late thirties, is the lover of Michael, a distinguished political leader and an exceptionally warm, intelligent man. Although they are now close, at the time Sandra began therapy, Michael restricted his emotional availability to her. He set rigid limits on the time they spent together and clung to his loveless marriage, convinced that his image as a stable, reliable character could not be sustained if he left his wife for another woman. At the beginning of their long affair Sandra told herself that it would only be temporary, because she could not imagine that someone she could see so rarely could be a satisfying partner for her. Gradually, however, Michael relaxed some of his limits, and they saw each other or telephoned each other almost every work day. Still, Michael was generally unavailable to her on weekends and holidays. Sandra experienced from Michael caring love such as she had never known before. In spite of his limits, he was able to provide her with the steady, deep, emotional satisfaction that had been missing in her relationships with her changeable mother, her emotionally distant father, and her other boyfriends.

Sandra came to therapy because of the conflict her loneliness caused her. She and Michael had been lovers for several years. Although his love for her was real and sustained and although their sexual relationship was gloriously fulfilling for both of them, she often experienced debilitating depression and painful headaches over the weekends and during holidays, when Michael was usually with his wife. His work took him away very often, too, and because he was careful to preserve his image of seriousness and stability before his colleagues and constituents and to protect his wife from the hurt she might feel if she should learn of his affair, he almost never took Sandra with him. This also made her angry and sad. She found that no amount of reassurance from Michael that he loved and needed her could dissuade her from thinking obsessively about leaving the relationship to find another lover who, she imagined, would be around more often.

Sandra's psychological situation is complicated, but her "loneliness" is hardly uncommon. Many women "in love" feel they "need" to be with their lovers more than men believe that they "need" to be with their girlfriends. I think one reason for this is that as girls they are taught that the possession of a man is so important that as women they confuse the importance of loving with their need to have a man to display to the world. Sandra discovered in therapy that much of her "depression" was a cover-up for anger toward her lover, which she was afraid to express. Her father could not tolerate hearing of her hurt and anger toward him for his emotional unavailability to her as a youngster, and ironically Michael had confided to Sandra not only that he detested and feared his wife's anger but that he had left his previous lover because she became "too depressed" by the limits he imposed on their relationship. It appeared to me that one of the unconscious reasons Sandra had selected Michael as a lover was that she knew he would discourage any expression of sadness or anger. She, too, was afraid of these feelings, afraid that if she did not always appear bright, cheerful, and satisfied, a loved man would abandon her for a more agreeable, less troublesome "playmate." She had learned that her father could not respond to dependency needs in women (partly because he could not take any woman's needs seriously), and she supposed that all men whom she loved would be as emotionally bankrupt as he.

As a result, Sandra rarely expressed her longing to her lover but turned it against herself. Every weekend she felt so much pain, mental and physical, that it seemed to her imperative that she make a decision to find a new lover even though she dearly loved Michael and had flourished in many ways during their long relationship. She told herself that the pain she felt was loneliness, and this seemed to justify her desire to leave the affair. "Everyone" agreed that she was foolish to stay in a relationship with a man who had a wife and many interests away from her. Her friends told her it must be possible to find someone who could be with her more often and more regularly—the culture's definition of a "real" relationship.

Sandra intensified the pain of weekends and holidays without Michael by making herself feel guilty. She had deeply desired the attention of her handsome and socially prominent father as she now craved Michael's, and she had always assumed that her father must be more attentive and giving to others than he was to her. This was no more true than her similar assumption that Michael gave more to his wife than he did to her. She punished herself for her jealousy and hostility toward both her mother and Michael's wife by giving herself pain and then telling herself that she would have to deprive herself of Michael's love to alleviate the pain (and punish him, as well as herself).

In therapy Sandra recognized some important truths. First of all, both her father and Michael placed strict limits on their availability to *all* people, including colleagues, friends, and family members. Both of these significant men in her life played the "star" game, placing themselves on the inside and *all* other people on the outside, longing to be where the "important" man was; and both men found it easy to assert their limits in relationships. Sandra realized that she was closer to Michael than any other human being had ever been, that he shared himself with her as he had never done with anyone else. She knew, too, that he valued her for her ability to help him break down the barriers to intimacy within himself as well as with another person. If she had not been so motivated by her early desire to reach her father, Sandra might never have been able to tolerate Michael's excessive remoteness early in their affair. Realizing that Michael was more accessible to her than he could be to anyone else, including his wife, and realizing that her father gave very little attention and support to her mother or anyone else helped Sandra to be less jealous. Since she did not need to be so hostile any more she did not need to give herself so much pain as punishment.

We next worked on Sandra's ability to experience her anger and hurt directly, rather than as "depression," and to communicate them to Michael. At first he tried to reason her out of these feelings by suggesting that she see her friends more often on weekends or that she work in therapy on her "neurotic" hurt. Finally, in desperation, she decided to act out her despair and frustration in a therapy session, playing both parts, herself and Michael. She cried very hard, telling "Michael" that she was so hurt and depressed by his periodic "abandonment" that she would have to leave him; in addition to her other "reasons," she said he wouldn't want her any more if he knew how angry she was with him. As she acted out Michael, however, she realized that, unlike her father, he would never desert her because of her anger. She knew that he loved and wanted her and that he would recognize that frustration and even sadness were only a small part of her feelings toward him. She also knew that she could trust Michael's resources, which were actually much greater than her father's. Furthermore, her ability to contact Michael emotionally was much greater than her ability as a rejected child to contact her isolating and isolated father.

Gradually Sandra began to tell Michael of her anger and hurt regarding his many absences from her. Because she no longer did this in a way that aroused his guilt, he responded with interest and warmth. Because she could share her feelings with Michael, Sandra no longer had to turn her pain against herself. Michael still could not bring himself to leave his wife and perhaps never would, but that had very little to do with his genuine love and need for Sandra.

One of the most important feminist aspects of this case was the difficulty Sandra experienced in setting limits for herself. Once she no longer needed to see herself as a pained victim of Michael's limits, she recognized that she herself wanted a less than total relationship. She had always loved to spend hours alone, playing in her house or reading and writing when she wasn't at work. Whenever she was involved with a lover who wanted to spend more time with her than she with him she found that she could not set limits to their contact, for she felt that she had to subordinate herself to the man's boundaries, whatever they might be. If Sandra felt very uncomfortable with whatever contact the man wanted she had to leave the relationship. This was one reason she had never been able to marry. In therapy Sandra learned that some of the limits she had attributed solely to Michael were also hers, yet she had previously been unable to acknowledge responsibility for them. When she was able to reclaim this projection of her own limits and learned to set them herself, with Michael and other friends, she felt more integrated and secure. This self-affirmation helped make it possible for her to enjoy her free time, which she actually valued. She could now relish her weekends alone instead of feeling pained and resentful. Eventually she began to publish some of her writing, a longed-for goal that she had at last freed herself to achieve.

I must add that Michael needed to know of her feelings; he needed to take into account the fact that she might indeed leave him some day for a more complete relationship. Sandra naturally felt better about herself when she was able to assert *her* realities and when she realized that she could not protect Michael from the effects of his own problems and did not want to do so. It soon became apparent that Michael was beginning to recognize that he, too, needed to take some responsibility for preserving their relationship if he valued it as much as he said he did. He eventually admitted to himself and to Sandra that his earlier "need" to restrict his emotional availability no longer seemed relevant to the relationship between them, if it ever had been. Sandra was never going to make him the center of her life as his wife and mother had tried to, so he had little reason to try to escape from her.

It would be hard to prove that women are more troubled by loneliness than men, but there are several aspects of loneliness in women that relate directly to our culture's values and expectations regarding women's behavior. Women, for example, are not expected to be as aggressive as men in seeking out sexual partners; therefore they experience greater humiliation than men when they do engage in frankly "predatory" activities as, for instance, when they go to a singles bar or to a resort looking for male companionship.

It's also true that women feel more pressure than men to have a companion of the opposite sex when they go out for an evening's entertainment, for there is first of all the cultural expectation for them (which does not exist in the same way for men) that they must prove their adequacy as people by showing that they are capable of winning a man. For women, this is the only important accomplishment required of them in adult life except for mothering a man's child. Second, women without male escorts are often not welcome in restaurants and bars.

Every woman alone reacts to her loneliness and to her aloneness in a unique way, depending on many factors in her background, her present situation, and her personality or character. When a patient says that loneliness is one of her important problems, I know that other strong feelings are involved and that these need to be clarified and examined in therapy. Exploring these concomitant emotions will help the patient to understand how she keeps herself lonely, for that is the most therapeutic question that can be asked about loneliness. (Many other questions might be important, but they are likely to be social-work issues, medical issues, or educational issues:

Does she know where to go to meet people? Is she physically able to get around? Does she have a phone?) If a woman is depressed simply because she is alone and is able to utilize other helpful interventions to end her loneliness, such as the services of a social worker, then she does not necessarily have a psychotherapeutic problem, for her depression should lift as she comes into contact with people who are potential friends. If she will not or cannot accept changes in her life that would make such social contact easier, she may need to work with a psychotherapist to understand what her isolation does for her and what she does to keep herself alone.

Among the important feelings that often accompany loneliness in women are anger and resentment. Since women are taught to be passive, they often feel (as do passive men, of course) that lovers or friends should come to them or "happen" to them; they do not perceive or accept the reality that one must actively create a loving situation, whether we are talking of love with or without sexual expression. From her earliest days, a little girl learns that she must wait. She may not aggressively go after what she wants. She must always wait to be chosen, wait to be asked to the party, wait to be asked to dance, wait for him to open the door or to get the car, wait to be touched, wait to be "given" an orgasm, wait to be asked to be *his* wife or lover rather than ask him to be *her* husband or lover.

(If I am grateful for anything in my own background it is that I learned from my mother two basic rules that have guided both of our lives. One is don't wait for what you want; go after it. The other is don't be a sheep and follow the flock; find your own way. Both attitudes have their own pitfalls when internalized as absolutes, but since I was incapable of following rules as given anyway, acting as if they were absolutes was never a problem for me.)

Sometimes along with loneliness a woman will feel

anger at a specific "rejecting" person, often a parent, a man, or one of her children. Since many women are taught to believe that others should be responsible for their welfare, the woman who perceives that her needs for contact are rejected may experience self-righteous anger at what she defines as the others' failure in their "duties" toward her. In general, society is sympathetic to women who construe their situation as abandonment through others' irresponsibilities.

A great deal of masochistic mileage can be squeezed out of the "victim" position (discussed more fully in a later chapter). When a woman perceives that she has been neglected or abandoned by her husband or her grown children or others, she may keep herself as miserable as possible in order to punish those who in her view are responsible for her bereft condition. If she is to choose to make a good life for herself she would have to give up the "right" to punish. At the back of her mind she may feel that if she were to prosper and enjoy life, she would reveal to the rejecting persons that she didn't need them so much after all, so whatever they "did" to her wasn't so bad either. That's a hard position for some "victims" to take, particularly those who derive much of their potency from their moral superiority. Unfortunately, many women have not been able to feel potent in other ways, so they push their "morality" on everyone. At least, they reason, God and right are on their side, and this reasoning helps give them the illusion of strength and control.

Psychotherapy can be tough going with neurotic "victims" who use their victimization to punish and control others. Obviously, the person whose feeling of worth is based on martyrdom and on an ability to arouse guilt in others has a powerful manipulative scheme underway. A woman can be just as invested in that sort of "proof" of potency as the sexual woman may be invested in and reassured of her potency solely by her ability to arouse men's sexual desires. Ultimately the therapeutic goal is to help such a lonely woman find ways of experiencing her effectiveness by achieving other valued goals, creating pleasant surroundings for herself, and developing mutually rewarding friendships rather than through her ability to arouse and play upon others' guilt in the service of her dependency needs.

A particular feminist issue in the psychotherapy of women's loneliness derives from the social pressure that is brought to bear on women to surround themselves with family life. Women are told from childhood that their social prestige depends upon their ability to attract a man, mother his children, and preside over his household. Most women therefore feel a sense of failure and shame, even humiliation, if they do not have such proof of their "adequacy."

The woman who feels worthless and humiliated because she is alone may need help to understand that these feelings arise in her because of the importance *she has learned* she must place on engagement in a love relationship and family-life functions. A feminist therapist will explore with her the possibilities for involving herself in other activities and relationships in which she can experience herself as worthwhile.

Another reason some women feel lonely is their too-narrow definition of a desirable solution to their state of aloneness. Girls are more supervised than boys in their choices of friends, and it follows that women feel more restricted than men do about the people they select as companions. It is not unusual for a psychotherapist to encounter women patients who describe their painful loneliness but in the same breath give all the reasons why this or that group of available people is not a suitable source of friends or lovers. It is still not usual for women to choose friends or lovers who come from a different social class than theirs or who are younger or less educated than they. Women need to allow themselves to be much more adventurous than they have been and to try out friends or lovers from groups of which their parents might not have approved. (Men have always felt much more free to roam around and experiment with "strangers.")

Another feminist aspect of this problem is the insistence of many lonely women that the proper intimate for them can only be an unmarried member of the opposite sex—that is, a potential husband. Again, this narrowness of definition is derived from women's overvaluation of a husband as the answer to all their problems, aloneness included. Many, many women hold tenaciously to the fantasy that since society says the best thing for them is a husband and family, this must be what they need in order to feel less lonely and more secure. It seldom works that way.

Living with another person has many lonely aspects, sometimes even more than living alone, for it means often that you have allowed yourself to be dependent on the other person to make you less lonely, and when he or she doesn't come through you are lost. I think the least lonely people are those who do not limit their definition of who or what will solve their problems of being alone but who leave themselves open to explore whatever a new friend or activity can offer. If you can be accepting of whatever a new person or animal or plant can provide without concentrating on and overemphasizing what it cannot provide in terms of your fantasies of the ideal love object, a feeling of pleasurable involvement usually follows.

Whatever solution to aloneness a woman chooses, she cannot rely on her learned passivity if she wishes to create a rewarding interpersonal situation. She must be active in seeking out many different types of relationships, and she must make demands of them that will make her happy as well as be giving herself. I would like to see women re-examine their prejudices against living alone, for many women could find ample happiness in the friendships they already have if they didn't feel pressured by the culture to have a single, live-in sexual relationship. Such a relationship may in fact *not* make an adult woman happier, and by concentrating on getting such a relationship for herself she may be neglecting the development of her inner resources and self-esteem as an autonomous, self-fulfilled person.

Nor does living alone preclude having a deeply gratifying love relationship, as is demonstrated by the situation of Sandra and Michael. As people become more able to resist the cultural convention of "man-wife" relationships and as more women are able and willing to be economically self-sufficient, it may be that more and more lovers will choose to live apart. Many couples, married and unmarried, are beginning to realize that there may be advantages in having a committed relationship in which each partner nevertheless maintains a separate household. Aloneness does not have to mean loneliness, depression, or anxiety. It can mean pleasure in oneself, time for diverse activities, and freedom to develop different kinds of relatedness with new people, with pets, with new ideas, and so on.

7

Depression

ELLY: *"He keeps telling me he's going to leave me."*

Like many young women, Elly came to therapy because of a depression, which she thought was caused by an unhappy love affair. It turned out, however, that, like many depressions, this was part of a lifelong pattern of reacting to frustration with despair, self-abasement, and the refusal to give up a bad thing.

Elly's family background provided a perfect setting for nurturing self-derogatory feelings. Her parents were always at odds, insulting each other and refusing to speak at all for long periods of time. Elly's mother was uninvolved with the world beyond her home and suspicious of the intentions of all but family members. Her chief concern was that Elly and her younger sister should behave themselves and not arouse neighbors' criticisms. From her mother Elly learned that others are ready to be hostile to women who do not placate and ingratiate and that there should be nothing more important in life to a woman than the opinions of those around her.

The natural insecurity Elly felt as a child because of the presence of a younger sister was heightened by the especially intense feelings of rivalry and inferiority generated in both girls by their mother, who made invidious comparisons between them whenever she thought one or the other needed special "motivation." Since their freedom was restricted in many ways, their standards of behavior were limited to what their mother thought was right; the sisters had little opportunity to observe the behavior of others, and what they did observe was usually criticized as inferior or evil by their mother.

In Elly's search for love and for uncritical acceptance, this attractive and capable young woman attached herself to Mark, a young man whom she described as passive and dependent. Their relationship had been going on for six years when I first saw Elly. She thought she was depressed because the relationship seemed stagnant and because Mark, annoyed by her constant demand for more attention and more love, threatened to leave her and find someone else.

A typical interaction might begin with a telephone call from Elly to Mark. In tears, she would claim that she was lonely and didn't know what to do with herself, and she would beg him to see her. He would then stay on the phone with her, "helping" her to feel better, for as long as two or three hours, during which he would insult her and make her feel worse—by telling her for example, that he never wanted to see her again. She would finally hang up, feeling abandoned. Ten minutes later she would feel furious at him, call him up again, and scold him. Mark would then agree to see her over the coming weekend. Sometimes he would keep the date; often he wouldn't but would call and say that he didn't want to see her. When they did meet, Elly would always sleep with him, knowing that sex was something he relied on. From Elly's description, it seems that Mark felt sexually insecure. Whenever he failed to get an erection with Elly he would tell her that what he needed was variety in women, thus threatening her in an area where she felt particularly insecure: competition with other women. An important part of their relationship involved Elly's gifts of services and money to Mark. In addition to sexual accommodation she "serviced" him by running errands, lending him money, and doing secretarial chores for him. Elly was an efficient and well-paid businesswoman, much respected by her colleagues. Mark, on the other hand, rarely had work and piled up debts, depending on Elly to bail him out by lending him money or by writing placating letters to his creditors. Elly made herself readily available, hoping that as a result Mark would assure her of her unique value to him.

Theirs was a typical "sadomasochistic" relationship. They alternated roles, but Mark was more often the "sadist" and Elly the "female masochist." Like many women involved in such absurdities, she was "loyal" to him to the point of caricature, refusing to get involved with any activities or friends unrelated to him. She had narrowed her social world to this one man and thus could feel intensely angry and resentful when he couldn't and wouldn't come through for her. "You're all I've got" was her message, and the hostility in it is obvious.

Elly claimed that the relationship was making her unhappy, but members of her therapy group noticed that very often when she described how Mark would come around for his handouts, she smiled. Clearly it was necessary for her to recognize the *power* she derived from his dependency on her. She needed to see that power and the struggle for power she and Mark were engaged in were more important to her at this time than the love she thought she craved.

Eventually Elly could no longer ignore her intense involvement with power and control in her relationships at work, with group members, and with me. When she could not control others' reactions to her and when she did not get from them whatever she wanted, she would react with sullenness, frustration, and depression. She got very angry at anyone who balked her, and in no way did her expression of anger reduce her depression. (That's a nice theory, but it had no relevance to Elly's real experience.) What was more important was Elly's recognition that she was acting just like her mother, whom she perceived to be the "strongest" member of the family. In order to be "strong" like mother, Elly reasoned, she would have to be resentful, throw temper tantrums that scared others into compliance, and show her associates how they were destroying her happiness by their failure to meet her wishes and "needs" as she perceived them.

To exercise power in intimate relationships is one way that women can feel potent, since they are not encouraged to pursue or express power in the outside world. But Elly had no real need to restrict herself to a world as narrow as her mother's. She began to accept as healthy the need for some power and control and to seek these in places where she could do herself and her employer some good. She also realized that others have rights, too, and she learned in her interaction in the group that intimacy with friends was as gratifying as feeling powerful through manipulating others. Eventually she lost interest in Mark when she recognized his loveless exploitation of her and no longer needed his dependency to make her feel potent. The group provided her with a context for values and behavior much more varied than those she grew up with. From the other women in the group Elly learned that a relationship with a man is only one of the many interesting and gratifying relationships available. She also learned from all the people in the group that she was by no means uniquely persecuted by fate in having a disappointing love affair.

When women come to treatment for depression it is usually because of a perceived failure in intimate relationships; when men are depressed it is usually because of "failure" in their work (or at least that's what they say). Most psychotherapists agree that women appear more often than men for treatment for depression and more often for depression than for any other psychological problem. Some psychological investigators assert that men are depressed as frequently as women, but that since women are culturally permitted to express feelings of need, sadness, and helplessness and men are not, men must mask their depressed feelings by physical illness, which is treated medically.

Although it may be true that men's depression often takes physical forms, my view is that women *are* more often depressed than men, for many reasons. For one thing, depression is a condition that is certainly aggravated if not actually engendered by the influence of sex hormones on the pituitary gland, which in turn produces other hormones, particularly norepinephrine, present in the body at high levels in depression. This produces a vicious circle, since depression itself seems to raise levels of norepinephrine and in addition diminishes the body's efficient utilization of vitamins, particularly the B vitamins. The common physical response of the body to depression is to conserve energy, which makes sense since the energy is needed for one's defense against illness and outside stress, both physical and psychological. This is the reason for the feeling of apathy that most people experience when they are depressed, and it is why they are more susceptible when depressed to the viruses that are always around. Getting sick, in turn, further depletes one's resources for taking the actions that are necessary to correct frustrating life situations.

Sex-hormone influences have been crucially implicated in the notorious depressions of some women at such significant developmental events as menarche, childbirth, and menopause. Currently, however, most people attribute these depressions to women's negative attitudes toward the new roles resulting from these life-style changes. Even many feminists say that depression at menopause, for example, is due to a woman's loss of self-esteem because she can no longer produce children. They go on to say that if she had other goals for herself that were supported by society, as motherhood is, she would not be depressed.

I disagree. I think psychological attitudes are important at all stages of life, but I believe that the chief cause of distress at these significant periods is a change in hormone level and not in sex role. To overemphasize women's feelings about themselves as the source of their troubles is once again to reinforce women's inclination to blame themselves for everything. It would be better for feminists to demand that women's (generally male) doctors treat their depressions and other complaints seriously, as medical problems to be solved, and that they prescribe hormone medication where indicated and encourage efforts to discover and make available new preparations that would be helpful.

A very curious and devastating thing happens to some people when they are not feeling up to par physically and/or psychologically. They make a terribly destructive and totally erroneous connection between "I *feel* bad" and "I *am* bad." I think women do this more often than men because they are taught to take so much responsibility for the tensions and unhappiness of the most important people in their lives. Traditionally it is the task of women to make everyone "feel good," even where this is patently impossible. So women "internalize" and feel it's somehow their fault if they and others feel terrible. I have heard many women patients (whose symptoms may or may not be psychosomatic) state that they are sure they are "doing something wrong" to be producing painful physical states for themselves. By blaming themselves for their own physical problems (and for others' tensions), women create in themselves the conditions fruitful for depression. Furthermore, they make it difficult to like themselves enough to feel worthy of good physical and psychological care. When a person says "I feel bad, therefore I *am* bad," she may then deprive herself of the self-love and comfort she needs to feel better. She feels worthless and undeserving, even of adequate medical attention.

How does a woman learn to feel this way? By being told over and over as a child that her illnesses and tensions were due to her "badness": "If you had worn your rubbers, you wouldn't have caught cold" or "God punishes little girls who talk back to their parents." To make matters worse, parents frequently feel unconscious guilt when their children are physically or emotionally distressed. They can't stand to admit that their children's problems may be their fault, so they project blame onto the child (as if blame were relevant).

I want to make a distinction here between taking responsibility in the existential sense and taking responsibility in the moral sense. I *do* believe (and it is the principal message of much of this book) that women need to take primary responsibility for making their lives happier. But that does not mean that women are *bad* because they are unhappy. When women are mildly depressed they should do what they can in the ways they know about to make themselves feel better. If they are physically ill, they need to assume *first* and not *last* that there may be a medical reason for their illness. They should allow themselves to rest without guilt and let the household take care of itself and of them too. If the depression is continuous and debilitating, *even if* there is a direct physiological condition underlying it such as recent childbirth or menopause or a serious physical illness, it is sensible and self-protective to seek psychological guidance. The crucial thing to do in illnesses of all kinds is to *get help*, no matter who or what one thinks is to "blame": a man, one's body, or one's well-proven tendency to fuck things up. If a woman feels bad, she deserves help. Her resources are under siege and they need reinforcement from the outside. Even if a woman who is depressed cannot give up the notion that she is "bad," she can assure herself that even "bad" people need help.

Another reason for women's depressions is that women have, or perceive that they have, fewer choices about what to do if things don't work out than men do. Psychological research indicates that both people and animals tend to react with depression when their avenues of escape from an intolerable situation are blocked. Society provides women with fewer choices of life-style and avenues for self-expression and achievement than men have. To make things worse, women are saddled with the moral as well as the physical responsibility for the care of young children, so that it is harder for them even to fantasize escape from their families much less actually to take a needed vacation.

Further, women are expected to adjust and make do and not to make waves about anything. They are expected to endure and be stoic while men are allowed to be assertive about trying out new ways; women are more often called irresponsible or flighty if they "run around" trying this or that to change their life situations. (If men move around and make changes, they are more likely to be called adventurous or courageous!)

Forbidden to move, some women get depressed, and the result often is that they literally can't move; often they can't even get out of bed; not happy, not "useful," certainly, but not a threat to anybody, either. People almost *expect* that women will be immobilized at some time during their lives, and literature is full of such heroines, both fictitious and real: Elizabeth Barrett Browning, for example, whose paralysis was almost certainly psychogenic. "Help me, I can't move" was the anguished cry of a number of the female characters in the movies of my childhood and adolescence. Of course the young doctor arrives, falls in love with the "victim," and either cures her before he marries her or promises to take care of her lovingly for the rest of her life. A number of fairytale girls were immobilized in one way or another, too. There was Sleeping Beauty, of course, and we all know how she was "awakened." Snow White kept poisoning herself with the witch's apples and combs and falling into paralyzed stupors from which she was saved by all kinds of males, from The Prince to the outrageous ugly dwarfs who made a slave out of her, forcing her to keep house for them and to cheer them up. (Ordinary woman's work, of course, even to this very day.) The point is that, for some nutty reason, our culture almost obliges a woman to be flat on her back at some time in her life, incapable of getting up on her own steam and out of whatever destructive situation she is in. If she does escape, she must do so with the magical help of a male agent, who then promptly indentures her. If she doesn't get up and out, well, who cares anyway? She looks very pretty lying there!

It is also true that women are permitted by our culture to romanticize sadness, longing, and dependency more than men are. They have learned that it is appropriate for them to be sad and to feel helpless without a "protector." To this extent they may be "taught" to choose depression as one way of reacting to troublesome situations.

By far the major reason more women are depressed than men is that they feel more guilty about being angry than men do. Depression is a punishment to the self and an angry communication to significant others. The chief task in the therapy of depressed people is to help them express anger and hostility in a way that can bring about needed changes in an unsatisfying situation. Usually the depressed woman feels so guilty about her anger or dissatisfaction (she has been taught to have only beautiful feelings and to adjust to unpleasant circumstances) that she punishes herself with painful feelings of unworthiness and hopelessness. Unfortunately, depression causes the sufferer to withdraw and therefore is not useful in getting satisfaction from the world.

One of the most exciting aspects of helping depressed patients in therapy is tracing out with them all the many ways in which they have learned to act "depressed" instead of openly angry; thus they sustain an image of themselves as impotent and deprived, trapped and hopeless. Depressed people often come to therapy thinking that if they receive love, support, and "supplies" in the form of advice, compliments, or reassurance from the therapist they will no longer feel sad. The therapist who provides only these things for depressed patients is not usually helpful and might well be insincere. Chronically depressed people can be a drag to their therapists just as they are to their friends. They have a way of ignoring any help that is offered or complaining that the offering isn't enough. They are often convinced that people in the "helping" professions owe them something simply because they have chosen to enter these professions, and so they may become more depressed (really, more angry) when their demands for more care or comfort aren't met. Sometimes their anger is expressed indirectly, in the form of a suicide attempt or threat or by some other ostentatious behavior that is meant to expose as publicly as possible the therapist's perceived cruelty and ineptness.

I believe it is appropriate for a therapist to show as much anger as he or she feels toward a depressed patient who is provocative. If the therapist is a woman and the depressed patient is a woman, the angry therapist serves as a model for a woman's being able to express anger. I disagree with therapists who try to provide depressed patients with the kind of all-giving mother that no one ever had. It is more useful for a depressed woman to learn how to express anger and how she keeps herself depressed.

She may discover, for example, that when she asks for advice, comfort, or reassurance, she puts much more energy and emotion into the request than into listening to the answer. Thus, she is likely not to notice when she receives the "supply" she wanted or to forget it in an instant and ask for the same thing a few minutes later.

She may exaggerate the sad aspects of her existence and ignore or denigrate the good things about herself and her life. Life for all of us is not a cup that is *either* half full or half empty; it is always *both at the same time*. The depressed person sees only that the cup is half empty and doesn't recognize the extreme danger to herself of ignoring the fact that it is also half full.

A depressed woman may tend to fixate on one person as magically designated to provide her with what she thinks she needs to "feel better," ignoring the other resources available to her, including her own. This is evident over and over again when a depressed woman is in a group. Sometimes it is the group leader whom she wants as her supplier, but often it's another patient who she imagines to be better off than herself. If her "magic supplier" lets her down she will sulk or be angry for a long time, forgetting or ignoring the presence of as many as twelve other people who might be able to offer her *something* and forgetting how much she can offer herself.

I feel that group therapy is so valuable to depressed patients that I will occasionally make attendance in a group (mine or someone else's) a condition of treatment. The reasons for making such a condition are to help the depressed person learn to spread out her attachments and to provide her with a laboratory for seeing how she restricts her awareness of the sources of gratification that are patently available and thus maintains her depression. (Many depressed people hang onto the determination to get what they want from their one "special" object for years, totally blocking out of awareness the many other people and involvements available to them. In the midst of plenty they behave as if they were in the Great Depression. Exactly.) A group also will provide plenty of situations that will provoke anger in anyone, including depressed people. And the depressed person must learn to express anger rather than depress herself with her "bad" feelings.

As I mentioned earlier in this chapter, the depressed woman often equates "I feel bad" with "I *am* bad," an attitude that prevents her from getting for herself the best life has to offer. She maintains a picture of herself that seems to justify ill treatment, but no one treats a depressed person more cruelly than herself.

Further, a depressed woman may believe that men should be "stronger" than women, and when they are not she feels that her failure to get what she wants from them (and from anyone else who she is convinced is better off than she) is due to her own personal unworthiness or lack of skill. It is very hard for a depressed person to recognize that even the people magically designated by her to be her helpers and suppliers are only imperfect human beings with limits and needs of their own. If they do not respond to her wants, it may be because she turns them off. It may also be because they are not able to meet her demands.

Very often a depressed person chooses a partner who is also depressed. They may validate each other's view of the world as ungiving and each other's expectation that others "luckier" than they *should* be responsible for them. They may have very little to give each other or be too angry to give. A woman such as Elly, who was attached to a depressed and dependent man, may feel "stronger" than he from time to time, and this makes her feel better about herself for a brief period, but she again feels deprived in possessing such an "ungiving" partner and fears that she may be unable to attract anyone better. One of the most deleterious results of a woman's attaching herself to a depressed man is that she may jettison many of her own strengths in order to maintain the illusion that her male partner is more adequate than she and thus is theoretically capable of protecting her and providing for her, as she has learned that men "should" be. When she is asked to describe herself before she became attached to this particular man she will almost always note that she lived more fully and with more of a sense of her own competence than she now does. Helping her to be in touch with these "former" strengths makes her feel more potent and less hopeless about the future. Obviously, a feminist-oriented therapist would help her question her expectation that men ought to be stronger and more capable than she and would help her assert her own strengths.

The depressed woman often adamantly rejects opportunities to connect with those aspects of herself that are aggressive and managerial. Like Elly, the depressed woman often will try to control a dependent man by making sex, money, and/or nurturance available to him, not perceiving that this behavior helps to keep the man dependent on her and unmotivated to do things for himself or for her. Elly had no awareness that her over-protectiveness and unwillingness to say no to any of Mark's demands represented a way of controlling him and assuring that he would return to her whenever he thought he needed something. She only wanted to see herself as dependent on him and "desperate" whenever he threatened to leave her. But obviously he wasn't going to leave. She had succeeded in making life so easy for him that he kept coming around for his handouts. Still, she couldn't or wouldn't see herself as by far the stronger person in that relationship, displaying all kinds of creativity and skill in keeping him around.

Depressed people always believe that nearly everyone is better off than they are. They spend a great deal of energy noticing what others seem to have that they don't. Suppressed competitiveness is common among depressed women. If they feel particularly guilty about competing, they turn their own healthy competitiveness into indignation about the "grabby" behavior of others who do compete. Such women have generally been taught that little girls should withdraw from competition; yet they may reveal their competitiveness by the comparisons they draw between themselves and others, usually to their material disadvantage but moral benefit. Everyone else has more luck than they, they think, but they are by far the "nicer" people, undeserving of the bad deal they receive from life.

To such a woman, self-assertion and competition for its own sake are repugnant, unthinkable, and morally inferior. Again, there is no better therapy than group therapy for her. She needs to see that one of the ways she maintains her depression is by withdrawing from the opportunity to win something when others also want something.

The best way to prevent depression in girls and young women is to help them relieve themselves of guilt for the parts of themselves they perceive as bad—generally anger, hostility, or dissatisfaction toward those perceived to be "authorities" or "superiors." Depressed females have usually been taught as little girls to be lovely, nice, good, compliant, accepting, and respectful. They have been trained to ignore or to pretend to ignore the anger, hostility, and meanness of others toward them and their own toward others and to believe that most people, particularly those whom they have been taught to respect or admire, mean only well. They cannot, therefore, believe that their own or others' ill feelings are ever quite real or justified. Thus, they need help from a therapist in perceiving and labeling their own and others' hostility (rather than ignoring or rationalizing it). In this way contact and communication can be maintained and problems more easily resolved than if the person withdraws into a sulk to express her anger or hurt feelings.

This view demands that therapists, too, own up to their hostility or anger toward depressed patients when it occurs, for to deny it only reinforces the patients' notion that "authority" or "helping" figures don't ever do anything bad, so if one feels hurt and angry at the therapist it must be because one's own head is on wrong. That way nothing unpleasant ever gets discussed or fixed.

8

Common Transference Patterns

Transference is the term Freud coined to describe a patient's feelings about, attitudes toward, and views of his or her analyst, which largely determine the patient's behavior toward the therapist and what the patient accomplishes in therapy. For many patients, therapy becomes so personalized that the patient cannot adequately separate the therapeutic process from the person of the therapist. For example, a patient may think that coming late does something bad to the therapist, and the patient therefore expects a scolding, whereas his lateness is not necessarily destructive to the therapist (although it may interfere with the therapist's desire to work hard with this patient). Similarly, when a therapist says, "I think you should come twice a week instead of once a week; how do you feel about that?" a patient may answer, "I'm happy because if you want to see me more often you must like me."

In classical psychoanalysis, where the therapist tries

not to disclose his personality, tastes, and values to the patient, the patient's views regarding these characteristics of the analyst are likely to be distorted projections of the patient's expectations, "transferred" from his past encounters with authority or "expert" figures. Therein, thought Freud, lay the value of the analyst's keeping himself or herself undisclosed to the patient. Freud's reasoning was that the patient would be forced to "project" his necessarily distorted view (of authority figures in particular) upon the person of the analyst, and that these distortions would be thrown into bold relief against (Freud hoped) what the analyst knew to be true of himself. Clarification of these distortions would help the patient to understand and correct his misperceptions not only regarding the therapist and therapy but also regarding his emotionally involving relationships outside of therapy. Freud's correct assumption was that people do act with internal consistency and that, consequently, one of the most significant tasks of therapy is to help the patient bring into sharp focus his *patterns* of thought, feelings, and behavior—in a sense, vividly to "map out" his personality. A therapy session may begin with the feelings and acts that arise in the therapy hour, but frequent questions are "Where else do you feel this way? Can you describe another situation where you experienced feelings like these?"

Modern therapists know that they need not remain so hidden from their patients as Freud thought necessary in order to elicit transference, for no matter how much or how little we reveal ourselves to another, whether as patient and therapist, teacher and pupil, friend and friend, or lover and lover, most of us tend to look upon the other and interpret the other's behavior as much in terms we have learned from our past as in terms of the other person's reality.

Some therapists believe that most patients are at a

disadvantage in determining whether their attitudes toward the therapist are distortions or not. They reason that where the therapist does not want to admit a particularly unfavorable characteristic is his, he can confuse the patient's reality testing by denying this characteristic and claiming that the patient's view is a misperception. This undoubtedly happens at least occasionally in everyone's therapy, for no matter how well therapists know themselves and how undefensive they are about most of their personality characteristics and behavior, it is reasonable to expect that particularly perceptive or hostile patients will find something to point out about therapists that will elicit a hasty and firm denial; sometimes therapists will deliberately lie about possessing a certain characteristic, and sometimes they are really unaware of it in themselves.

The question is not whether therapists hide their "real" selves from patients, but whether it is necessarily harmful to the patient for them to do so. My feeling is that unless the therapist is quite sadistic and intent upon driving the patient more crazy than he or she already is, in the service of maintaining the therapist's own grossly distorted self-image, it probably is not harmful to the patient if the therapist occasionally ignores the patient's assessment, particularly if the patient's comment can be used to help her learn something about herself.

That this is feasible derives from our modern view that transference is not merely a matter of distortions and that analyzing the transference does not mean only, or even most importantly, determining whether the patient's view of the analyst is distorted. If the therapist is a "soother," for example, the way the patient's mother was a "soother," and if the patient's attitude toward the therapist's "soothing" operations is like her attitudes toward her mother's soothing, we might say that the patient's *perception* is realistic insofar as she has correctly interpreted her therapist's gestures as "soothing." But it is still transference if her *attitude* toward the therapist's behavior came from her past experience with her mother. Suppose the patient's response toward the therapist's soothing is to grow angry and say something like "You want me to be a baby!" That interpretation and the anger that goes with it come from the past, even if the therapist *is* like the patient's mother and *does* want her to be a baby. It is a transference.

The proof of this is that another patient exposed to exactly the same soothing behavior may respond with "Gee, I really feel comfortable here." Neither of these responses is any "better" than the other. The point is that they are both products of these patients' pasts, *as is the fact that such behavior on the part of the therapist has been selected as important enough to be noticed and remarked upon by the patient at all.*

Either response indicates that the patient is still involved in dependency issues, and *that* is more important than whether the patient is correct or incorrect in discerning the therapist's behavior and motivations. The first response is a rebellion against dependency; the second, an acceptance of it. A response that would be more or less not a transference would be one such as: "I notice you seem to think I need more support than I do, so I feel your soothing attitude toward me has more to do with you than it does with me. I want you to know where I really am." The constant correction of others' distortions regarding ourselves is part of the serious business of bringing about rewarding relationships for ourselves, and the therapeutic relationship need not be an exception.

If the patient points out a characteristic of the therapist and the therapist neither confirms nor denies it but, rather, asks, "Why does this come up now?" the therapist may be appropriately (not defensively) drawing the patient's attention away from the therapist's personality and trying to get the patient to focus on why a (possible) characteristic of the therapist has now become important to the patient. What the therapist is, in effect, asking is: "What difference does this aspect of my personality make to you *just now*?" Of course, I am not saying that it is never appropriate for a patient to criticize a therapist or to ask him or her to change. *It is always appropriate to bring to the therapist's attention anything about the therapist or about the therapeutic procedure that one experiences as hurtful or bewildering.*

Since men and women have somewhat different socialization experiences regarding authority figures, they naturally display somewhat different transference behavior. The most common transference patterns of women to their therapists reflect their most significant interpersonal orientations: feeling impotent in relation to another whom they perceive as more powerful; being "passive" and awaiting direction; and feeling insecure and seeking protection, assurance, and approval. With a male therapist, some women also utilize a pattern of attempting to experience power by eliciting the therapist's sexual interest.

When people in therapy are challenged regarding behavior that expresses the feelings they hold about themselves, they typically become anxious or angry. These feelings are expressed in and out of therapy in a variety of ways, unique to each person. Women in particular have learned to express anxiety by becoming more "helpless," "fragile," and dependent; by acting "emotional"; by being self-righteous and scornful of the other person or persons in the interaction. Women often express anger indirectly, by criticizing the other, clamming up, or bad-mouthing the offender to outsiders. Sometimes they internalize the anger, becoming depressed, physically reactive (developing illnesses, such as insomnia, headaches, skin problems), or self-abusive (taking drugs, overeating, overdrinking, getting pregnant and having an abortion or an unwanted child, or causing others to hurt them physically or emotionally).

Feelings of Impotence

Patients who are members of one of society's oppressed groups—and these include women—frequently feel that the therapist, even if she is a woman, is more "powerful" than they. Their experience has been to idealize and exaggerate the power held by others in relation to them and to make themselves unaware of their own potency. Sometimes being unaware of one's own power has a certain survival value, for a powerless person cannot be a real threat to others; we "play dead" to dissuade others from attacking us. In therapy, however, as in most life situations, this attitude is clearly inappropriate; worse, it is destructive to self-esteem and to any chance of attaining more real power.

Sometimes people come to think of themselves as powerless because they define *power* too narrowly—for example, in terms of money or political clout. In any case, it is an illusion to think that the therapist (or anyone else) has *all* the power and the patient has none. Unfortunately, patients are often out of touch with their own *uses of power* and unaware (usually) of how they give up their power to another. Patients may express power in relation to the therapist, for example, by hiring and then firing him or her; by coming to appointments late or not at all, making the therapist wait around instead of being able to run off to the laundromat; by not paying on time, if ever;

making frequent changes in their appointment schedule; by threatening to kill themselves (and sometimes doing it); by getting arrested and asking the therapist to intercede; by acting generally helpless. Once patients get the therapist involved, they may then reject him or her for being too political or too nonpolitical, too young or too old, too rigid or too flexible. They get the therapist to worry about them and to discuss them in his or her own supervision or peer-group sessions. They get the therapist to write books about their problems because they are so "interesting" or enigmatic or anxiety-provoking. They express power by talking about the therapist to the therapist's other patients and to other therapists.

Not only does the therapist not have "all" the power, but she or he is committed to helping patients learn how they make themselves powerless. How patients do this and how they keep themselves unaware of their power—which they not only have but exercise all the time, one way or another, in relation to the therapist and to others in their lives—constitute much of what the patient and therapist work on together.

When their uses of power are revealed to them and when they become aware of how they overestimate others' power or make themselves powerless, people from oppressed groups frequently feel much better about themselves and may then be readier to take on the task of achieving more power in the economic and political spheres, where they do indeed have little power in relation to truly powerful and oppressive others.

The therapist has the responsibility to help patients see where they do have power and how they use it unawares. This is best done as the patient spontaneously exhibits her power to the therapist, as happened, for example, in a memorable session with one of my patients.

GINA: *"Nobody pays any attention to me."*

After a particularly bad day at work, Gina arrived at my office, as she frequently did in those days, in a depressed and passive mood. She often felt ineffective, like a cipher and would complain, "Nobody pays any attention to me." When Gina was in a mood like that, totally unaware of her real effect on others, she could become very abusive and rejecting of whatever attention anyone paid her. That had been a down day for me too. My son had recently gone to another city to live, and I was missing him. As Gina was describing her depression and sense of ineffectiveness, instead of being analytic I tried to cheer her up (as I wanted to be cheered up, probably). She rejected every optimistic remark I made, and when I finally shut up for a moment and became more analytic, she told me how stupid my attempts were. In response to a comment of mine that I thought was particularly keen, she said, "Well, that certainly sounds like something out of the *Readers' Digest.*"

This was simply more "rejection" than I could take at that time. I felt furious and said so. In the next second I realized that I was going to cry. What to do? I had never before cried in front of a patient in response to an attack on me, although I had cried a little from time to time in response to something sad or moving that a patient had said about her own experiences. Since it was apparent to me that I was not going to be able *not* to cry, I decided to use the incident as well as I could to make a therapeutic point. There was little for me to say. Gina saw exactly how effective she had been, just how powerful she really was in relation to her therapist. She had hurt me, as she hurt many people in her life, all the while thinking that "they" have all the power.

I cried for a few minutes; there wasn't anything else I

could do. Then we both nervously laughed a little and talked about what had happened. Gina said that for the first time she felt really "grounded." She was very appropriately regretful that she had hurt me, for she likes me (as I like her), and she was shocked and I guess a little pleased that she could do something so effective to another person. After my tears were over, I said, "Wow, this is some therapy!" Gina (who had had several previous therapists) said, "Well, it certainly is different!" If there is such a thing as a turning point in therapy, that session was it. Gina could never again claim that patients —women—"victims" have no power, or that therapists (authorities) cannot be moved.

BETSY: *"Perhaps he'll like me better if I let him think he's more competent than I am."*

An example of how a woman may "act out" feelings of impotence as a part of her transference occurred in a session that I had with my supervisor, David. I had been discussing with him my patient, Julie, who was critical of me and dissatisfied with her therapy (as well as with most other interactions in her life). She had called me one day to scold me for the hundredth time and to say again that she wanted to stop therapy. Instead of feeling threatened and helpless as I often did with her, I reacted more securely in this particular conversation and managed to lead her to some important insights about herself. She really decided to stay in therapy and work. I felt very satisfied with the interaction on the phone and pleased with my new confidence and skill with her, which I knew was in large part the result of the hard work I was doing with David. I could hardly wait to see him to describe how I had been able to react more competently with this patient. There was one part of the phone conversation of which I was particularly proud, and I went over and over it in my mind on my way to my supervisory session, eager for David's approval.

Eagerly, I began to tell him what had happened. But, as I was approaching my most triumphant moment, I realized that I had forgotten the crucial details. There I sat, feeling exposed and helpless while he was waiting for me to recount this marvelous incident. I had just demonstrated my feelings of "incompetence" by forgetting what had been the best example of my competence in a very difficult transaction with a patient.

David is my own age and in my eyes a skillful therapist and a "successful" man. At one time he was my own therapist, and I then had to confront again and again the feelings of inferiority and incompetence I experienced in his presence until they were mostly worked through. In supervision, long after my therapy was finished, I reverted to my old feelings. If David had asked me then, "What's good about that?" my answer would have been something like: "It reminds me that a man will protect me and rescue me from my own fuck-ups if he thinks he's more able than I. Perhaps he'll like me better if I let him think he's more competent than I am." The focus for me was David's competence, not my own, and that is certainly a common transference pattern of women: to focus on the male's "adequacy" rather than on their own. One might also say that I "sacrificed" my own feeling of potency in order to "give" David the opportunity to feel like a rescuer, a consoler, so that he could feel big and strong. Then he said, "You don't have to act that out with me," and I remembered my lost scene. By his telling me that I didn't have to be a helpless little girl with him, I suppose I felt "permitted" to act more competently. At that point it would have been appropriate for me to examine why I needed permission and how I got him to give it to me.

Passive Behavior

Passivity is a learned behavior that serves important purposes for a great many women at certain times. Men also behave passively in many circumstances, but generally speaking they do not receive approval for passive behavior, as women do, particularly in relation to the opposite sex. Among the many ways in which women act passively in and out of the therapy room is through their verbal abilities.

JUNE: *"How can I change?"*

Using her great skills in abstract thinking and verbalization, June tried to convince herself and me that she was working on her problems, "figuring" them out, and attempting to "outsmart" them. But it was all head-work and mouth-work—like her approach to dieting, for instance. June was too fat for her health's sake and for the attractive appearance she highly valued. She was unhappy in part because she was not attractive. Like many "passive" people, she first tried to blame others for her unhappiness. If "society" would alter its standards of beauty, then she wouldn't feel so inferior. Notice that June's energy here was directed toward getting *others* to change.

I asked her point-blank, "Look, if you're so unhappy about your looks, how is it you don't do something about making yourself look better?" Faced with such a question, "passive" verbal people really go into action. They have bushels of answers. First June explained why my question was stupid: Any fool knows that losing weight isn't a simple matter of will power; many more complex factors are involved, and until every one of those factors has been isolated, "understood," articulated, and *treated* (by the "doctor"), she can hardly be expected to go on a diet! (If I had been dumb enough to ask what those complex factors might be, enough verbiage would have resulted to occupy a hundred sessions and to postpone June's dieting a few more years.)

Fortunately from the point of view of therapy, June used the same ploys in other areas of her life about which she was dissatisfied; because she rarely took any direct action to change them, she was unhappy about many things. It is the pattern of passivity and how that pattern is maintained that the patient needs to recognize. When this pattern shows up in therapy it is an example of transference because the patient expects the therapist to accept the same rationalizations that important figures in the past accepted. She also reveals in her transference how she expects others to do things for her when she acts "passively." The "passive" person is very potent indeed!

For example, June was also distressed about her messy apartment. We decided to work on this problem. Here is June "working" on her messy apartment. First she said that when she was growing up her mother had been "too clean," and she wanted to talk about that and about her theories of "reaction-formation," thus ensuring further delay in cleaning up her apartment. Then she tried explaining how a clean apartment would not be "her," because she was a spontaneous person whose "real" personality was best expressed through a messy apartment.

"Well, okay, but who brought it up in the first place? I thought you said you weren't happy with your apartment?"

"I'm not, but that's because I learned from my subculture that apartments should be clean. If society would change its values about cleanliness, I'd be happier with my apartment."

"June, what are you doing now? Isn't this what you said about an attractive figure?"

"I guess I'm trying to give everybody else responsibility for where I am and what I want. Well, I agree that no matter where I learned these values, they are certainly mine now. I'm the only one who's suffering because I'm not living up to my expectations. I guess the choice is to make myself happier and work for what I want or to make a decision consciously not to work for it. I keep waiting for conditions to be more perfect or to understand myself better. I guess I really hope that you or 'knowledge' or 'insight' will change me. I see now that I'm kidding myself."

June's understanding of how she was using her verbal and intellectual ability didn't develop overnight. We had to explore every area in which she was dissatisfied and go through the same process of inquiry until she caught on to her own manipulations. And they were not only manipulations of me, for, as June said, she was kidding herself. Like most passive people, she was trying everything before owning up to the fact that she was unhappy with herself and that if she wanted to be happier she was going to have to take action in spite of whatever discomfort and deprivation that might entail.

June's "passivity" in the our relationship could be seen primarily in her "good girl" compliance. She was always "reasonable"—that is, she never displayed anger or rebellion in our sessions or asked to change anything about the emotional climate or the time or money arrangements of therapy. She never expressed any dissatisfaction with me but, rather, "went along." When we investigated her compliance she said that she was taught as a child that a girl never gets what she wants by being temperamental or by asking directly. She was told, rather, that "good" girls are rewarded and that girls who "make waves" (ask for something *they* want) will never have their wishes granted. Many girls learn "passivity" and manipulation in this way. June was told in childhood that her mother and an aunt, who frequently cared for her, were people who had "problems," and this was a further reason not to "upset" them by "making a fuss." Asserting herself or arguing with the grown-ups was considered "making a fuss." Her aunt and mother had hit upon a perfect way to control and deprive her, first of all by lying to her (only "nice" girls get what they want), and, second, by telling her that she would be doing something destructive to them if she expressed emotion or an opinion different from theirs.

Another important way in which June expressed "passivity" in therapy was by asking many questions of the "why" and "what" variety. "Why do people behave like that?" "Why did she do it?" "Why do you think I do this?" "What can I do?" "What *else* can I do?" "What will happen if I don't do this or that?" These questions not only were expressive of her desire for guidance and reassurance but were ways of procrastinating.

A useful technique to use with ourselves when we discover that we are asking someone too many questions is to turn each question asked into a statement. "What do you think?" becomes "I think"; "Where are we going?" becomes "Where I am going is ..."; and so on. This helps us to recognize that not knowing all the answers is a part of everyone's real experience, and instead of being anxious about not knowing and running to an authority for answers we can risk thinking and acting on our own.

As a substitute for direct communication, June frequently constructed fancy, vague abstractions—the kind of thing college students write in response to essay questions on tests when they don't know enough facts—bullshit. Very often she really didn't know what she was talking about, and if *I* said something in turn that *she* didn't understand, she would swallow it rather than ask, "What do you mean?" This was another way in which June was passive in our relationship, harking back to the days when she never questioned the neurotic and controlling behavior of her mother and aunt, which the whole family rationalized as determined by those ladies' "problems." What *were* their "problems?" No one ever asked.

Another of the ways in which some women act "passively" in therapy is by becoming very anxious when the therapist does not direct the discussion. Sometimes this occurs at the beginning of the hour, when the patient arrives and says, "I don't have anything to work on today." Sometimes the patient runs out of steam in the course of the session. If the therapist knows that this patient habitually hangs back and waits for "others" to take the lead, then all the therapist has to do is resist her own temptation to go in there and "rescue" the patient. Any "helpful" question, such as "What are you thinking?" or "What's going on now?" or "Can't think of anything to say?" or "Are you feeling anxious?" will be gratefully appreciated. If the therapist *does* perform this rescue operation, she may be surprised to find that *now* the patient spills out a torrent of material. Where was all this a minute ago? Well, of course it was there, but since nobody asked for it, the patient wasn't about to offer it. The therapist was conned into performing the directive role that the "passive" person often gets others to play, and the patient was deprived of an opportunity to experience how anxious she feels when the responsibility for presenting material to work on is hers alone. This kind of interaction provides a good opportunity for the patient to learn that although her "passive" behavior doesn't permit her to display potency as it is usually defined, her ability to get others to play the roles she assigns them is an example of how powerful she really is.

Patients also act passively but powerfully in therapy by "playing dumb." When a woman is anxious, she may say to the therapist or to others in the therapy group, "I don't understand." So someone will make the last interpretation a little more clear (and simpleminded). Then the patient will say, "I still don't understand. Can you say that again?" So someone will say it a little more simply. Again, "I *still* don't get it." Finally it's time for someone to say, "Look, you've gotten us first to feed you adult food, then pablum, and now you want us to turn it into milk and pour it down. What's going on here?" One thing that's going on is the transference aspect of the interaction; getting others to force-feed her what she doesn't want anyway. She could have said the first time, "I'm not ready to hear what you have to tell me, so please don't help me with this now," or "I'll work on this myself later when I'm not so anxious." Either of those would be assertive statements.

One of the most self-destructive ways of being passive is with regard to our moods and strong emotions. Many women mistakenly believe that there is something almost sacred about feelings, and that when we feel something vividly we should give up every other faculty of our minds and let that mood hold sway. Thus a patient will say, "I couldn't sit down and do my English assignment because I was too depressed," or "I was so happy and it was such a beautiful day I decided just to enjoy my feelings." What's wrong with that? Sometimes a lot.

Some people have difficulty getting in touch with most of their emotions and need help in contacting and acting on almost all feelings. In my experience as a therapist, however, this is more often the case with men than women. Many of the women seen in therapy, by contrast, have been encouraged by society to experience and express and even to get lost in their feelings. While this has its pleasures, it also can be subversive, undermining women's progress toward influence and self-esteem.

There are, of course, certain feelings that women are not allowed to feel and act on, such as direct anger, competitive career strivings, and sexual desire; but other feelings, such as romantic love, helplessness, narcissism, confusion, nostalgia, and nurturance, are permitted and even encouraged in women and are acted out by those in therapy at various times in their transference. There the therapist has an excellent opportunity to observe women's "passivity" in relation to these feelings, which patients so often believe are beyond their control.

The two cultural attitudes that permit and encourage the tyranny of feelings in women are the notion that it's "feminine" to be emotional and the idea, a corruption of Freud's theory, that repression of strong feelings can lead to neurosis. Contemporary men and women probably need to acquire different stances toward emotion and emotional expressiveness: Men need to feel more free regarding their emotionality, and some women may need to value the ability to channel and focus their feelings, so that feelings can be used to guide action when appropriate, not only as an end in themselves.

That this is possible can be easily seen. If you were depressed and lying around in your room, "unable" to do anything, how would you behave if you saw smoke creeping under your door? Wouldn't you jump up and investigate? If so, what would have happened to your "incapacitating" depression? Obviously our minds have more faculties at any one time than the capacity for experiencing emotion; yet many people remain passive and allow themselves to be controlled by their emotions alone, even when this is destructive. Our capacity for enjoying our feelings and sharing them with others can enhance our pleasure in ourselves and in our relationships. But to get lost in a mood can also mean forgetting where we are going. Women in particular need to be suspicious of the "turned-on" philosophy that permeates the human-potential movement today. The way to women's liberation and political power will not be through the primal scream any more than through the emotional excesses of religious experience. If women want equality they will have to value and use their wills and their minds as well as their emotions.

Let me emphasize that I am advocating not repression of emotion (nonfeeling) but, rather, recognition of the value of controlling emotion; if we can control when and for how long we want to experience a particular emotion, we can use it to enhance experience, and we can turn it off when we want to direct our attention elsewhere.

A final word about "passivity." There is no such thing as a "passive person." Some people act in ways that we call passive in certain situations or at times when they feel anxious, helpless, or, frequently, angry. Many women have learned "passive" behavior from their culture because women are not readily permitted to respond directly to frustrating circumstances with either self-assertion or forceful anger.

To summarize, even so-called passive behavior can be very powerful in its effect on others; a woman's passivity may be very arousing to those in her immediate interpersonal arena. She may get others to do things for her, to give her advice, to support her procrastinations, to encourage her to place exaggerated blame on outside forces for her lack of achievement and her low self-esteem. She may readily arouse anger and guilt in others, which further attests to her potency, for others are rarely unaffected or indifferent to passive aggression.

The most valuable tool the therapist may have with regard to the transference "passivity" of such a patient is the therapist's own emotional reaction to the patient's various maneuvers. When expressed spontaneously and nonpunitively, the therapist's emotional response can sometimes underscore, as nothing else can, how powerful this so-called passive person really is. Thus it can be an important step toward her growth. The therapist, of course, should be sensitive to the patient's need to feel potent and should use her own reaction in the spirit of "Look what you are capable of doing!" not "Look how destructive and terrible you are!"

The Need for Approval

Men seem to have many more sources of approval of themselves than women do, and I believe it is that fact, not the "fact" that men more easily "internalize" feelings of self-worth, that makes women seem to be more dependent on outside sources of approval. Men, for example, are likely to derive feelings of self-esteem from the social status and professional prestige they have earned for themselves, while most women derive their status from the achievements of their fathers and husbands. Men can accrue feelings of competency from doing difficult work that is valued by society, while women's "work" is generally housework and child care, which can be done quite skillfully even by poorly educated and immature women. Men can make contributions to their fields and to society that are recognized by a large impersonal public. They may be in their offices making their reputations while their wives are at home making the baby smell good.

I got that message one morning about twenty-five years ago when it suddenly occurred to me that my lover was in his office writing one of the books that made him rich and famous at the very same moment I was sitting in bed writing him a love poem. In twenty-five years, would he be as dependent on me for his self-esteem as I would be on him? Hardly. So I got out of bed and went to school.

Even if a woman's lover is not rich and famous, the point is valid that he has a better chance of feeling good about himself without her than she has without him, or without his constant reassurance. Many women come to therapy in the first place because they are not currently attached to a loved person who they imagine can provide them with the self-esteem they need, either because they do not have a close attachment at all or because their hoped-for source of support is less than supportive. Women patients therefore are much more likely than men to set the therapist up in their minds as a source of assurance that they are "okay." Women who come to a feminist-oriented therapist are often very distressed by their dependence on a close personal attachment as a source of approval, and they hope through the help of the therapist to liberate themselves from the attitude expressed so well in the song:

> Sometimes I'm happy, sometimes I'm blue,
> My disposition depends on you.

They would like to be able to generate not only more self-approval but also self-approval that is not rooted solely in how their love lives are going.

An important responsibility of a therapist who is aware of feminist goals is to help women live up to their ideals in this respect by showing them how even in transference they are exhibiting their need for approval from an important "other." One of the ways in which this can be accomplished is for the therapist to ask the patient who is describing some action of hers, "How did you feel about yourself when you did that?" It is vital for any therapist working with women to be aware of the subtle ways in which they may ask for approval, and it is crucial for a woman's growth that her therapist resist the temptation to act as a powerful approval-giving figure for her. Women need to learn to use their opinions of themselves as guidelines for behavior and as reinforcement, not the opinions of special persons whom they set up as their arbiters. Therapists also need to help such patients become aware of how they ask others to perform this function for them, and of how they may limit their out-side sources of approval so that the therapist or another important person becomes the only source.

It's unrealistic to expect people to be totally inde-pendent of the opinions of others. Since we are all in-terpersonal beings, we are concerned, not necessarily neurotically, about the impression we make on others, and it is appropriate that we be aware of how our actions affect others, regardless of whether we want to change anything about ourselves as a result. At the same time, it is desirable to have many sources of this information.

I believe that one of the greatest problems for women is not that they are dependent on outside sources for approval (because everyone is, to some extent) but that they tend to limit these sources to one or two intimate attachments and then to idealize and overvalue these persons. The end result too often is that the woman defers to this idealized "other" and sacrifices much of her autonomy and emotional expressiveness in the service of placating the other, constantly courting his or her favorable attention. Those who are in the position of the all-important approver usually resent this role even if they are flattered by it, for they recognize how crucial their good opinion is to the other and thus feel pressured to restrain their disapproval or anger even where these feelings are eminently justified.

A climate that permits free expression of negative as well as positive feelings is the right of every human being in all his or her relationships. Sooner or later, a person who feels that his negative expressions are "inappropriate" or destructive to the other seeks a way out. This is true in the transference relationship too. If the therapist permits the patient to idealize her and set her up as the sole or most important source of assurance about herself, the therapist may be colluding in what will be the patient's abortive termination of therapy, for the patient may eventually feel so unsatisfied that she will flee. For the sake of her therapy as well as all her other endeavors, the woman patient needs to expand her sources of self-esteem and especially to learn how to be one of those sources for herself—ideally, the most important one. If liberation means freedom from enslavement, this is one of the most important kinds of liberation: the freedom that accompanies knowing that one can pretty well sustain good feelings about oneself and about one's life even when other important people are not consistently present or supportive.

The Controlling Mother

MARTIE: *"Mother knows best."*

As a reaction to deeply buried feelings of inferiority and impotence, some women act out the role of controlling mother. Martie, a middle-aged mother of four, felt very threatened by the idea that she might need help with her problems. She preferred to see herself as totally self-sufficient and all-knowing. She said she wanted therapy only to get someone on her side in her constant battles with her children. Because it was very important to Martie to feel like an omniscient mother it was practically impossible to say anything about her children that did not agree fully with *her* interpretation of their motives and needs. As if this wasn't enough, she also offered her interpretations of *my* children's needs!

Naturally she tried to make me one of her children, too, although I am about her own age. She began therapy by assuring me that she could come to sessions during the day so that I wouldn't have to work at night, even though I had offered her an evening appointment. When I told her what my fee was she magnanimously explained how I could pad my bill so that her insurance company would pay me even more than I had asked. She started every session by asking how *I* was and then stating exactly what she wanted to work on, what the "real" problem was, as she saw it, and what she wanted the outcome to be. If I asked her to look at a person, a problem, or an event in a different way, she reacted as though I were a well-meaning but dim-witted child. Totally unwilling to give up control of the subject being discussed, she would launch into a honey-toned expansion of her original point of view.

One day I asked her in a friendly and reasonable way if she thought she needed therapy. She said, "Yes, but I'm not very receptive to it." I told her that I felt useless because she hadn't changed and her life was no better than it was at the time she started therapy. "It seems to me," I said, "that you know exactly what's best for you and for everyone in your life. What could you possibly learn from someone who knows less than you?" To my surprise she suddenly began to cry very hard and very genuinely. She protested that she was indeed very unhappy and that she saw no way out of her misery unless she gave up the illusion that she could run the world perfectly. She admitted that, since it was evident to her that she had fucked herself up, maybe mother doesn't always know best. Then, gingerly, she began to respond to therapy, and she was able to consider the viewpoints of others without fearing that to do so meant that she would necessarily be proved "wrong" and therefore affirmed in her unconscious perception of herself as inferior. From that point on, her relationships began to improve.

9

Defensive Roles Many Women Play

"Defenses" or "defense mechanisms" are the psychological attitudes and behavior people use to ward off anxiety. For example, rationalization (the process of assigning an apparently logical but untrue reason for one's behavior or feelings rather than admitting to oneself the "real" reason) saves us from the anxiety of recognizing a part of ourselves that we prefer not to know about.

Defenses are often used by patients in therapy as resistance to change. Since an important goal of therapy is to help people recognize aspects of themselves that they have pushed out of awareness and take responsibility for those aspects ("own" them), the process of therapy is largely concerned with identifying the "defense mechanisms" and showing the patient, or helping her to see for herself, how she uses them to obscure her recognition of a significant but anxiety-provoking part of herself. Again, the ideal goal is for the patient (or any person) to be able to say, "I recognize that feeling or that act as an important part of my personality, and I no longer have to act as if it doesn't belong to me or come under my control."

The "Victim" Defense

All people are able to some extent to act as free and responsible agents and at the same time, are to some extent true victims of various circumstances that prevent them from assuming as much responsibility in their own behalf as they might wish. Nevertheless, some groups are more discriminated against than others in their attempts to achieve self-responsibility and self-realization. They are real victims—that is a fact—and their inability to act freely in their own interests may be almost entirely the result of discouragement or actual obstruction by forces outside themselves.

Women are certainly members of such an oppressed group. The psychotherapy of women therefore has to deal with the psychological effects of true victimization, such as low self-esteem and feelings of helplessness. It must also, however, deal with the use of this real victimization by some women as a defense against recognizing whatever is their own responsibility for the place where they are in their lives. Without both a sense of responsibility and a feeling of potency, no "victim" can hope to change her situation.

In my experience, the patient who uses the victim defense characteristically comes from a family of society's traditional victims—Jews, blacks, and other minority groups, including, occasionally, a family in which at least one member is significantly handicapped physically. Most parents in such families meet their children's attempts at self-expression with a combination of pes-

simism and envy. Very often the parents become extremely angry when one of the children tries to be
"different." Their anger probably expresses their fear
that a deviant child will further isolate them from the
community's values.

This is frequently the case when a girl in such a family
dares to be other than invisible—that is, compliant, self-
sacrificing, and sexually subdued. If she attracts attention for any kind of "deviant" behavior, she has to deal
with her family's anger and her own consequent guilt
and fear. (It is not unusual for a child who expresses a
tendency to be different to become the family scapegoat—a convenient displacement for their feelings of
disappointment and resentment at society's rejection.)
The girl thus learns from her own family that she is their
victim as they are society's, and she is thus doubly victimized, as perhaps many people are who come from this
type of family. As a child she learns many "victim"
behaviors as preferred defense mechanisms, among
them the romanticization of victimhood and the use of
"projection" ("I'm not bad, they are bad to me") and
rationalization ("If it weren't for them, I wouldn't be so
screwed up"; "They won't let me be happy and successful"). The true victim is often expressing an attitude well
founded in her actual past experience. Not only was (and
is) society stacking the cards against her self-fulfillment,
but if she is more successful, more accepted than her
parents, she may have to deal with their jealousy and
suspicion as well.

If such a feeling is realistically derived from a woman's
actual circumstances, then why treat it in therapy as if it
were a neurotic defense? The answer is that it can be a
realistic attitude and at the same time a self-destructive
one. It is crucial for the feminist therapist to help patients
to make this distinction.

Therapists and patients can identify the use of victimization as a defense in at least two ways. One is to gauge the amount of energy the patient has invested in herself as a "victim" in relation to the amount of energy invested in activities and attitudes that would be more conducive to changing her image of herself and her life circumstances. The other important way is to explore with the patient the advantage she derives from seeing herself as a victim.

Dramatic shifts in energy expenditure often occur when a woman is finally ready to relinquish the neurotic use of her victimhood. Rebecca, the divorced mother discussed in Chapter 2, spent two years bitching about the (real) difficulties of rearing a child alone when she had no training for a job she liked and nothing in her previous social conditioning had alerted her to the desirability of preparing herself for single life. Finally she gave all this up and within a short time discovered that the obsessively drawn, wildly colorful doodles she had produced during her angry moods had commercial value. She now pours her energy into contacting buyers; creating new ideas for clever and lucrative uses for her doodles, on textiles, wallpaper, toilet paper, greeting cards, notepaper, et cetera; and carrying her money to the bank. Now that she's no longer bitching, does she still doodle? Yes. The ability hasn't left her, but the motivation is different. She is, however, still a woman and therefore to some extent still a true victim, but because she *feels* more potent and because she has given herself more social power, she is less available for victimization.

Victims' Benefits

A good measure of the extent to which a particular woman is using her victimization as a defense is the amount of anger with which she greets any attempt in therapy to explore the advantages she derives from seeing herself as a victim and projecting this view of herself to others. Many women and other real victims will leave therapy unless they feel that the therapist is sensitive to their actual victimization and the pain ensuing from that. This is as it should be, but once the patient can trust that the therapist is genuinely sympathetic to the real injustices she has suffered, she may be ready to explore some of the hidden gains in thinking of herself as a victim. What we want to look at in therapy is her unconscious use of certain of these advantages to keep herself in the very circumstances she professes to hate.

An important advantage of being a victim is the excuse it provides for keeping oneself out of the rat race; if you don't see yourself as having to achieve in the same ways as members of the "preferred" group, you can afford to play around. You can give much greater expression to your potential for far-out activities. You can wear crazy clothes, try new life-styles, and in general, if you're not too depressed and angry, have a pretty good time— maybe in some ways a better time than society permits those from whom it expects conventional success. You can cop out if you want to, and that's not such a bad thing. The trouble comes if you want the same power, money, and public respect that members of the preferred group have, and you see no avenues open by which to secure them.

There are other benefits to the woman who elaborates her victim image. Some women (and other true victims) have fantasies of success and prestige that are greater than are realistic in terms of their intellectual capacities or their temperamental inclination to sustained effort. Here, obviously, victimhood can serve as a rationalization for one's not having achieved as much as one desires. Such a woman's therapy has to help her become more aware and accepting of her real limits and to see that the goals toward which she aspires may not be realistic for her. They may require an effort she would not want to make if she saw any other choice she could live with. Very often this woman has painfully high performance standards for herself and other people and would welcome a chance to let up if supported in this by her therapist.

Another common benefit of the victim defense is the sexual excitement the self-image of victim provides for some women, such as Barbara (Chapter 3), who could no longer feel sexually aroused after suppressing her masochistic fantasies.

Finally, victimization may provide an opportunity for self-pity and self-righteousness, a combination of feelings displayed by women characters in much romantic fiction. Not a few of us as adolescents stood before the bathroom mirror and watched the tears slide down our rosy cheeks as we conjured up images of ourselves as beautiful, wronged heroines. Some impressionable women, who were perhaps rewarded for that posture by their fathers or older brothers, learned to associate the ability to weep easily (and not too hard) with sexual desirability. In my experience as a therapist, the women who make this association have not known many real-life love and sexual relationships. They seem to be waiting for an illusory romantic figure who will kiss away their tears and rescue them from victimhood. They are still stuck on fairy tales.

As in the instance where sexual pleasure, actual or fantasized, accompanies the image of oneself as victim, therapy is difficult for women in this situation. They need to be helped to reveal their secret and romantic sexual wishes, about which they may feel foolish. These women need to see that they have developed and are choosing to retain a certain view of themselves because it provides some psychic benefits, even though it also prevents them from achieving a self-image that would help them to feel more potent.

Women Who Make Themselves Available for Victimization

I have pointed out that the best way to learn how a patient does anything outside the therapy room is to observe what she does inside. The patient who "makes herself available" for victimization, for example, often arrives late to her therapy appointment. Sometimes she has victimized herself, or let others do it for her, on the way to the therapist's and then imagines that the next patient victimizes her by arriving on time.

LINDA: *I let everyone take advantage of me."*

On her way to therapy one summer day, Linda, a young woman who was very simply dressed and looked as poor as she was, was stopped on the street by another young woman, a stranger, who said, "May I have a minute of your time?" Linda then *allowed herself* to be subjected to a rap from this girl about a religious group with which my patient was unfamiliar and in which she had no particular interest. She listened for ten minutes, in spite of her quickly approaching therapy hour, then turned to walk away. The girl then made a plea for a donation, saying that since Linda had listened so attentively, she must see the need for funds. That wasn't quite all. The young suppliant then asked Linda to distribute some leaflets for her group. Linda gave her some money and took the leaflets. She arrived fifteen minutes late to her appointment, furious at herself for having been a sucker, furious at the girl on the street, and furious that her therapy time was limited by the punctual arrival of the next patient.

In her session, we explored how she had made herself available for victimization. First of all, she saw herself as a victim and had identified with the financial "need" of the girl on the street and with her right to stop people who looked more fortunate than she. Since Linda couldn't have looked more fortunate than the girl who had stopped her, we had to examine her use of the situation to make herself feel more potent than the other girl. She was willing to make a choice—to sacrifice her therapy time in order to feel more powerful than someone else. But she didn't know that was the bargain. She also wasn't fully aware of how much gratification she got out of complaining about her victimization and the malevolence of others, which made her appear morally superior. Finally, by blinding herself to the choice she was making of her own free will, she made herself available for one final victimization—that of herself by herself. For doing a somewhat dumb thing she now blamed herself for committing a Terrible, Stupid, Self-Destructive Act.

Patients also make themselves available for victimization by not asking the therapist questions about who the therapist is, what his or her values are, and what he or she considers appropriate treatment goals. People who are frequent victims do not often take advantage of my asking, "What would you like to know about me?" in the first session, and they often romanticize trust. People who frequently "find" themselves victims may think that they are disarming the aggression they really expect by making themselves very "innocent" and "harmless." If a patient goes into a "victim" rap in the first session and then fails to take advantage of the opportunities given her to learn more about me or about therapy so that she might know what to expect and how to judge the appropriateness of my kind of therapy for her, I ask her first how she expects to be victimized by me and then how she could imagine victimizing me. The victimization she anticipates and often sets herself up for is frequently a projection of what she fantasizes she would do if she had the power she imagines that I have. Recognition that "even" a patient has the power to victimize the therapist is often enough to make her feel more comfortable and more in control than she thought she could be.

People also make themselves available for victimization by idealizing the potential victimizer. A certain hostile flattery is implied, ("I'm sure you're too good to take advantage of me"). Almost a cliché is the girl who dresses in hotpants and halter to go on the subway and then becomes indignant when she is stared at or pinched. Men *should be* better than that. But they aren't. One of my patients bragged for several sessions about how much money she was making in the nightclub business. When I raised her fee, she yelled. She was a victim of my greed! Not quite true. She had been seeing me at a reduced rate, and when she paraded her income in front of me I acted in my own interests. I'm only human. The payoff for the victim in these cases is the guilt the other person expresses when his or her "baser" qualities are exposed. The victim feels morally superior to the Lust, Greed, Envy, and other Deadly Sins expressed "against" her as she sees it. One might well ask here, who is the victim and who is the victimizer?

When the Therapist Is a Member of the Same Group as the Patient

It goes without saying that the "victim" may expect that

the therapist who shares her minority-group status will be supportive of her feelings of victimization. A woman may have chosen a woman therapist for that very reason. If the patient is using her victimization in neurotic ways and the therapist points this out, the patient may well feel betrayed and, of course, victimized. The therapist had better be prepared not only for the patient's anger and disappointment but also for her own "counter-transference" feelings—a real bundle of discomfort: Is the patient right in believing that the therapist is betraying one of her own kind? Is the therapist jealous of her patient for getting a more understanding therapy than was available when she herself was a patient? Is the therapist feeling like a miserable conformist while the patient seems to be a noble fighter? Is the therapist taking advantage of her patient's victimization to make money from her? Is she just one more victimizer in the patient's life?

If the therapist's answer to these questions is no, then why isn't she more "sympathetic" to her patient's complaints of victimization? How could the therapist suggest that the patient might be getting some useful mileage out of her very victimization, the one thing she believes she's so unhappy about and wants so much to change?

In the long run, overidentification with a patient destroys the therapist's effectiveness. If the therapist buys into her patient's fear and awe of the "oppressor," her certainty that *all* the forces that frustrate her lie outside herself, obviously the patient's feelings of helplessness and hopelessness will be reinforced. If they are to feel potent enough to bring about change, women (and other true victims) need to be able to take responsibility for their self-destructive uses of seeing themselves exclusively as "victims" and to recognize the ways in which they may make themselves unwittingly and unnecessarily available for victimization. As long as she exaggerates her oppressor's potency and minimizes her own, a woman is stuck in her unhappy circumstances and with an unnecessarily frustrating image of herself.

In addition to reinforcing feelings of helplessness in the victim-patient, the therapist who oversympathizes thus makes herself ineffective and her job unpleasant. She is making herself available for victimization by the patient. She can be no more than a dumping ground for the patient's anger and despair, and eventually she will feel as helpless as the patient. Furthermore, she deprives herself of the pleasure of doing therapy, which derives from actively helping the patient to outwit her own self-deceptions. If the therapist frequently feels impotent with "victim" patients, she may need to ask herself how she became the "victim" therapist. Is she adequately separating herself from her patient's dynamics?

Where patient and therapist share the same minority-group status, such as womanhood, the therapist may be especially likely to serve as a model for her patient. If the therapist feels comfortable with the notion that others of her group may do as well as or better than she has done, she can be a model for her patient without arousing competitive feelings or "castration" anxiety (the fear of punishment for displaying competency or success)—that is, if the therapist herself is free of competitive feelings or "castration" anxiety! While serving as a model, she must at the same time help the patient to differentiate herself from the therapist. Since all patients are in the process of forming their own identities, it will be destructive for even the most well-meaning therapist to suggest that the patient can be "just like" the therapist. That is neither a realistic nor a desirable therapeutic goal. The therapist needs to assure herself, too, that while she and her patients may be similar in certain respects, they are also different people. Difficulties can arise if the therapist wants to empathize with the patient and really has been subjected to similar life experiences. The therapist needs to let herself and her patients know that their ways of dealing with the problems that result from sex discrimination and other manifestations of society's pejorative attitudes toward women might be very different. Patients are usually relieved to discover that the therapist does not expect them to be just like the therapist. It is equally reassuring to female therapists to know that they don't have to be just like their female patients. We don't have to prove our sisterhood by identical attitudes or behavior, and patients are not really asking for that. They are asking for *therapy*.

The *"Scheherazade" Defense*

The teller of the tales in *The Arabian Nights,* Scheherazade, was an attractive young woman who, for a thousand and one nights, was threatened with murder by her cruel husband, the king. She saved her life, however, dispelled her husband's misogyny, won his lifelong devotion and admiration, and, in short, caused everybody to live happily ever after through her cleverness and dramatic skill at telling interesting, entertaining cliffhangers. Well, okay. In fiction anything can happen. In fact, women are often very good storytellers. Women are brought up to be verbal and ingratiating, and these two characteristics in combination may make them superb entertainers.

LAUREN: *"You'll never believe what happened!"*

Lauren, thirty-four, is a poet who came to me for therapy because of her anxiety and depression. She had several serious life problems: Her income was inadequate to her needs; she had no real home, living in one hotel room after another; she had no reliably supportive relationships but many brief sexual encounters and fly-by-night friendships. She had had many, many therapists, both male and female. She enjoyed associating with people who lived on the brink of danger, such as auto racers, gamblers, smugglers, and stunt pilots, people who created for themselves situations where at any moment they could be "caught" by "fate." Impermanence, chance, and risk were her constant themes.

In therapy, Lauren behaved as if, like Scheherazade's, her life literally depended on her ability to talk in an entertaining, highly dramatic way about her harrowing adventures and precarious circumstances. She was hovering at the edge of psychosis and was unable to perceive how she produced real danger for herself by inattention to her basic needs. If therapy was to be successful, it would be necessary at some point for her to connect solidly with the fact that her psychological and probably her physical survival depended on her ability to rearrange her life in such a way as to provide herself with more predictable resources.

Everyone needs resources such as money and friends to count on as protection and comfort when threatened by feelings of panic, isolation, or illness. Having resources that are predictable also helps people to avoid personality disorganization, for some reliability in the world outside ourselves helps us to feel stable about what is inside ourselves. When Lauren began therapy she was unable to see that her anxiety was an almost reasonable response to the totally disordered and unsafe life-style she had created for herself. Anyone who lived the way she did would have been anxious.

One of the ways Lauren prevented herself from recognizing her responsibility to herself and from experiencing the anxiety of being insecure was by telling stories that were guaranteed to interest and arouse people who were attracted by someone else's dangerous lifestyle. She realized that some people admired the "courage" with which she negotiated some of her more difficult adventures, and she also knew that people like a well-told story. By telling her stories dramatically and skillfully she bought off people's anxiety for her safety and their potential criticism of her life-style, for their criticism was not so much moral disapproval, as she liked to think, but an expression of the anxiety that is normally aroused in most people when they find themselves face to face with another human being who seems insufficiently self-protective.

It's also true that some of her listeners may have envied Lauren her ability to disregard the more mundane aspects of daily existence, and her stories, told apparently for the entertainment of her listeners, subtly worked to dissuade them from angry envy. It's interesting to speculate about Lauren's competitiveness, too, for one doesn't go about telling stories about one's bravery and disdain for bourgeois comforts unless one hopes to compare the relatively lackluster lives of the audience to the apparent excitement and richness of the life of the storyteller.

Obviously, there were many "reasons" for Lauren's storytelling. In my estimation, this skill served her primarily as a defense against the anxiety-producing recognition of her existential aloneness and responsibility for herself as well as against the expected disapproval of others for whatever inferiority she imagined she uniquely possessed, in addition to the inferiority she felt as a woman. It's noteworthy, in this last regard, that some of Lauren's exploits, such as motorcycle racing, were typical of the escapades of "adolescent" males. Lauren seemed to be moving as far as possible from what she really was, a woman in her thirties, without becoming overtly psychotic. She removed herself from identification with conventional adulthood as much as she could without risking hospitalization as a regressed "infantile" personality. She traveled only so far back as adolescent boyhood, which isn't so far from what our culture admires that it would draw undue attention to her as a "disturbed" person. Lauren left therapy rather than look at her defensive use of her storytelling. She felt it was all she had, and it was not enough for her that her dramatic and poetic abilities were real, a genuine skill that no one would question. She didn't trust that she could examine her neurotic use of this ability without losing her belief in herself as a poet. Her sense of self seemed to depend on these identifications, and I went after them too quickly, before she could trust me.

The "Dresden Doll" and "Waif" Defenses

One of the more common and powerful defenses of some women is their internalization of our culture's view of women as especially fragile. According to this view, women are more vulnerable than men to feelings of rejection, to uncomfortable living arrangements, to hard work, to exploitation. They need to be "protected" from sadness, hurt, confusion, and anxiety by some "concerned-parent" figure. The message conveyed by the woman who employs this defense is "I'm fragile and not very practical, so please don't let anything terrible happen to me." She leaves it up to whoever is playing the role of concerned parent to protect her from danger, not so much because she thinks she is helpless (although that's a part of her self image) as because she thinks of herself as terribly breakable, very easily hurt.

Men are not the only ones who are willing to buy this

rap from women. Many women in the helping professions (who should know better from their knowledge
of their own power) believe that some women need more
protection, more comfort, more kid-gloves handling
than they really do. Something in the personalities of
many therapists, teachers, social workers, and other such
"parent-surrogates" finds gratification in playing Big
Daddy or Big Mommy. "Gee, somebody needs us" is part
of that gratification, but other aspects of it are less
attractive: "Boy, am I smarter than she is!" (to be able to
see danger in where she's heading), "I'd better let her
know how smart I am," or "Wow, am I a sensitive and
kindly helper; I'll bet *everybody else* takes advantage of this
vulnerable doll," or "Life was hard for me, but maybe she
can't take hard knocks the way I did, so I'll be very gentle
(the way I wish somebody had been for me). Life
shouldn't be so hard for us dolls."

A similar defense often used in combination with the
Dresden-doll defense is the waif defense. The major
difference between the two is in the appearances of the
women who are using them. The "doll" *looks* like a doll:
rigid, "cute," and often "sexy" in a stereotyped way:
pointy brassiere, tight sweater, short skirts, high heels,
big-eye makeup. She does not look sensual, however, for
she is too "dolled up" to imply a relaxed, natural
earthiness. Both the "doll" and the "waif" are typically
dressed as if they were ten years younger than they really
are. The "doll" looks either like a teenybopper without
rhythm or like one of Louisa May Alcott's "little women."
The "waif" looks like one thing only: an orphan straight
from an institution: no makeup, *ever*, no display of
figure, drab clothes, and scuffed, flat-heeled shoes. She
rarely wears slacks, and if she does they are shapeless
overalls. She looks depressed. The "doll" often is depressed too, but she hides this under a bright, though
forced and brittle, exterior.

Like the "doll," the "waif" believes that others should protect her from the normal hardships of living, for she too believes that she will blow away in a storm. "Please be careful of me" is the major message of both women.

OLLIE: *"I just can't work in group without crying."*

Ollie, a small-boned, pretty woman in her early twenties, came to therapy looking as if she had just got off the bus from the orphanage. She was dressed in a loose brown jumper that she had made herself; dark brown, opaque tights; and brown, flat-heeled shoes with a Mary Jane strap across the instep, just like Orphan Annie's. Her face was pale, and her long, lanky hair just hung there. She spoke so softly during her first session that it was impossible to hear a word she was saying; when I asked her to let her words reach me, she burst into tears and thereafter cried whenever she was asked to repeat a word or to speak up a little. She was saying, "I won't do anything you ask me to," but this sturdy resistance came out as "I can't; I'm too little." Ollie came to therapy because she was very isolated. She acted as if she was terrified of contact with people, and she really believed that she would fall apart on the spot if she had to talk to a new person. When, from time to time, she did meet someone new, in an art class or where she worked as a filing clerk, she would warn him or her that she was afraid of people and of getting "involved." She would also forewarn anyone who approached her that she might cry at any moment if she found the interaction too demanding. You can imagine how attractive people found that! After Ollie had been in individual therapy for a few months it became apparent to both of us that she should join a group so that she might learn to have more confidence in herself with others, to decrease her sense of social isolation, and to make it possible for both of us to explore in a laboratory situation just how she kept people away from her.

She agreed to join the group (continuing with her individual therapy as well), but for many weeks she didn't say a word. Finally she decided to work on a problem in the group, but she managed to cry so often and to speak so softly and in such vague terms that she frustrated everyone there. In the months I had worked with Ollie on our own, I had felt some of the frustrations that the group members expressed, but I had not told her of my impatience because I was oversold on her "need" for understanding and protection.

While I was secretly glad that most of the members of the group could express to Ollie the anger that I inhibited, I also felt that she would be so upset that she would certainly leave. Wrong. Ollie was furious that the others hadn't bought into her woebegone style, and instead of melting away she yelled right back at them in a focused, well-defined display of anger. Now she could no longer claim to be the vague, bewildered, unwanted child who could barely negotiate the complexities of human interaction. At least not in the group.

In her individual sessions, however, Ollie clung to the technique of confusion and tearfulness and the teeny-tiny voice until I no longer responded to her at all. In truth, I couldn't hear her. Instead of asking her to speak up, I let her go unheard. She finally noticed that I couldn't participate in her sessions because I really couldn't hear her. When she recognized that, she made the attempt to reach me. She was beginning to realize that *she* had the responsibility of either making therapy work or deciding and admitting that she didn't want therapy. She decided to stay in both individual and group therapy, and she put herself in a position where others could reach her and help her. This meant that she had to speak so that they could hear her, to offer a problem so that they could comment, and to absorb and respond to their participation rather than use their comments as stimuli for feelings of rejection and vulnerability. Ollie also recognized that by previously frustrating the group's desire to be helpful to her, she was (potently) trying to make them feel as helpless as she felt. It was important that she recognize just how effective she was in doing that.

This situation illustrates the usefulness of group therapy for the *therapist* as well as the patient. Not only do patients find it helpful to see how distorted their attitudes toward their therapist may be when they are exposed to the reality testing offered by many pairs of eyes, but the therapist, too, gets a chance to see the patient from perspectives other than her own. All therapists can benefit from having their perceptions of their patients validated, modified, or challenged by others in a group, and many a therapeutic impasse has been broken by a meaningful group session.

It is not only that new attitudes toward the patient form for the therapist as a result of seeing the patient as a group member. Because the group members function as cotherapists, they are able to add interpretations that are different from the therapist's. No therapist is comfortable enough or aware enough to supply everything that could be useful to the patient. For example, I tend to be cautious about patients who seem to be shy or withdrawn. My tendency is to "let them alone" and permit them to withdraw, which may be a projection of my need to protect (maybe overprotect) my own ego boundaries. In a group, some members are likely to feel no such need, and several patients in my groups have been, like Ollie, challenged in of their "shyness" by the vigorous attempts of group members to "intrude" themselves into territory that I felt to be sacrosanct to the patient.

"Ms. Charm"

Most of us are so envious of the charming, poised woman that we seldom ask ourselves any questions about how these characteristics came about or how they are being used. Our culture places great value on the woman who is an extrovert in a social gathering, who can apparently fit in with ease and draw others' admiring attention with her good looks and graceful social manner. In actuality, however, it is appropriate to be somewhat uneasy and withholding with those one doesn't yet know. We sometimes sense something undiscriminating about a person who treats all newcomers with equal graciousness, even though graciousness is a value women are taught to believe is desirable. We are supposed to be either a "perfect hostess" or a "perfect guest." We are supposed to make people feel comfortable and to suppress whatever needs for distance we may have and all our anxieties in the service of making others feel "at home."

When working with patients who are very charming and poised I have often been struck by their inability to come into contact with their own anxiety in situations that would make others uncomfortable. I feel that for several reasons "Ms. Charm" is a very difficult patient to treat. The main reason for this difficulty is that her particular mechanism for allaying anxiety, like that of Scheherazade, has won her so much social approval and is considered so desirable by admiring others that it has been, if anything, overlearned by the patient. The defensive use of charm has two significant self-destructive effects for the patient: first, the inability to perceive danger signals in close relationships, and, second, the inability to set long-term goals and to work hard to reach them.

With regard to the first, "Ms. Charm" expects and

works only to be appreciated and admired, no matter how hostile, anxious, or ambivalent she really feels. Much of her energy seems to be focused on getting initial approval or reinforcement, "setting up" her image with regard to both social and work situations. Once she has secured that initial reinforcement, she often has little drive left to apply to keeping the social relationship or the work project going.

For the charming, poised patient, anxiety is a feeling to be warded off at all costs, for she feels that the appearance of anxiety ruins the "nice" effect she is trying to have on others. Indeed, she relies for her identity and security on the "reflected image," and for her the whole operation is a deadly, vicious circle. It means that in therapy, for example, she cannot come too close to the areas that make her upset and anxious, for she fears that she will "lose control": to her, that usually means that she may cry or sob or simply have to admit that things are not going well with her.

People who are reacting spontaneously and authentically in therapy or anywhere else are not often behaving in ways that our culture describes as poised and charming. They may be trembling with terror or with excitement, they may stutter with anxiety, weep with rage or pleasure. They may turn away abruptly and unceremoniously from an unwanted encounter or move awkwardly, aggressively, or shyly toward one that is desired. A woman who feels truly secure cares more about being in contact with her own feelings, even those that are unpleasant and ugly, than about showing others that she is able to "keep her cool" at all times.

"Ms. Charm" frequently leaves therapy when she is asked to think about the things that upset her and to make contact with her anxiety. She may become extremely angry at the therapist for insisting on calling her attention to the projects she does not finish and to the friends who have defected or whom she has deserted. She is often unable to go beyond the initial-impression stage of a relationship, including the therapy relationship.

If "Ms. Charm" comes into group therapy, she is likely to arouse intense feelings in other group members, some of whom, particularly those who are awkward and shy, may feel great admiration and envy toward her. Others may resent what they regard as her attempt to manipulate them. One of the most shocking and meaningful experiences "Ms. Charm" can encounter is a group's refusal to let her make them "at home." It comes as a tremendous surprise to her that not all people need to be charmed out of feelings and experiences that are downright unpleasant and uncomfortable. If she can stay long enough in therapy, this patient needs desperately to know that she can be accepted for herself, or even rejected for herself; that, as a matter of fact, authenticity in behavior toward herself (admitting all her feelings) and toward others is much more satisfying and reassuring than social acceptance and admiration.

10

Brief Notes

The Phobic Woman

The two major classes of phobia are object phobias, which are feelings of panic and avoidance focused on creatures or things, such as insects, dogs, or jellyfish, and situational phobias, which are focused on locations or surroundings, such as open spaces, closed spaces, crowds, or great heights. It is believed that the incidence of situational phobias is greater among women than among men, and greater among married women than among single women. The oldest theory offered to explain the greater incidence of situational phobias among married women states that such phobias occur in women who both desire and fear the sexual temptation present in the world outside their homes. According to this theory, the danger of succumbing to the temptation is inside themselves, but they project this fear onto the situation outside, developing a strong anxiety about

157

some aspect of the outside world that conveniently inhibits them from going forth except in the company of their husbands, children, or their own mothers, any of whom would serve as a deterrent against temptation.

This is a very limited explanation of so complex a dynamic, and it does not take into account the effects of a woman's socialization on her tendency to develop a situational phobia, except for the obvious suggestion that women are inclined to feel guiltier about extramarital sex than most men because of the prohibitions they have learned regarding sexual assertion in general and sex outside of marriage in particular. I believe, however, that there are other, more important feminist issues in situational phobias, the most crucial of which is the conflict between dependence and independence. I developed such a phobia myself a few years ago and will describe it here to illustrate what I mean.

My daughter was five months old when she, my husband, and I went to stay for our usual summer month on Cape Cod with my husband's father. The weather was cold and rainy the whole month, so that I could hardly ever get outside with the baby. My father-in-law and my husband were, however, undeterred by cold and damp. They skin-dived in the rain, played tennis for hours in the fog, and hiked on the beach, generally leaving me, as I saw it, to shift for myself. Our tensions grew greater and greater until, desperate for some relief, I suggested that the baby, my husband, and I take the ferry to Nantucket, two hours away, to visit my son, who was staying there with mutual friends. My idea was to get myself out of my husband's family's house, where I felt I was being treated like an alien, and find some kind of refuge with my son. I urged my husband to come along with the baby and me for a change of scene. As it happened, he had another tennis date that he didn't want to break, and he encouraged me to take my little vacation by myself, leaving the baby in his care so that I could be entirely free to enjoy myself on Nantucket.

I was caught in a bind, for I didn't want to leave him and the baby, my two strongest attachments, but I didn't want to stay in such a tense situation either. I was ashamed of my "dependency." I could hardly believe that I—supposedly "mature," a competent professional, well analyzed, and all the rest of it—was afraid to go to Nantucket "all by myself." What kind of sissy was I to "need" to stay so close to my husband and baby? Thus denigrating myself all the while, I put myself on the ferry, wondering at the same time exactly what I was doing there. Nantucket Sound was rough, and I grew increasingly seasick, although I had taken preventive medication. I became more and more panicky, certain that I would vomit in front of everyone. I didn't, but the panic and many of its physical symptoms, such as sweating and nausea, persisted long after I debarked. With despair I recognized that I was having a classic anxiety attack.

For a few months thereafter I refused to go out alone. I was afraid to teach, which I had previously loved, because I told myself I was "afraid" to be "so far" from home in case I should "get sick." To make matters more difficult, my former analyst, whom I saw as soon as we got back to New York, died suddenly soon after we resumed our sessions. I was very frightened, for I genuinely couldn't understand why I was having such severe anxiety about leaving my house, and on top of that the person I relied on most to "cure" me suddenly was dead. Although I myself taught psychology and in-tellectually "knew" a good deal about anxiety states and phobias, I pretended to myself that I didn't know what was happening. This uncertainty made me all the more self-deprecating and afraid, for I thought I should be able to understand myself perfectly and by so doing somehow "control" my feelings and behavior. Instead I felt bewildered and depressed.

I called the institute with which my late analyst was affiliated and was referred to a man who was much younger and much less protective than my former analyst. I was so "afraid" by now of my mental "incapacity," whatever that might prove to be, that I "couldn't" even go to his office for the first time without being accompanied by my husband. Once there, I began to describe my phobic symptoms in glorious detail to my new doctor. This perceptive man interrupted me almost at the outset of my narrative by saying, "I don't want to hear about your symptoms, just tell me what's wrong with your marriage." He added, "People who have symptoms like yours frequently are whitewashing their marriages." In six months my symptoms were completely gone, and I have never suffered a recurrence.

My life and my attitudes toward autonomy for myself have greatly changed in the years since then. One of the most basic changes is that I have resolved my leftover resentment at not having parent figures to support me as they would a little girl. I can now accept the fact that my independent life-style is my own choice, not the result of rejection by people (including my own parents), whom I wanted to serve as my caretakers. My professional life is very different also, much closer to what I like, yet would not choose years ago. At that time I was impressed by academic status and wanted to become a full professor although I did not have the temperament for carrying out research projects or writing impersonal papers and articles. Eventually I gave up the goal of academic success and settled down to a private practice and to writing subjectively, which are much more emotionally gratifying to me.

This change was satisfying in another important way. It meant that I could stay close to home and my little daughter in a self-respecting way rather than having to get "sick" to do it. My closest personal attachments are very important to me and I like to be near them. I am indifferent to the idea of going to Nantucket, either literally or figuratively. Instead of pretending or wishing to be a different kind of woman than I am and punishing myself for "failing" to be this ideal self, I can better recognize and respect my own limits and desires.

The excellent therapy I was able to have at that crucial time helped me to become strong enough to face the real problems in my marriage, which I had been afraid to confront previously. The possibility that this second marriage might break up and that I might once again have the sole care of a young child was very frightening to me. The marriage did break up, as it should have done, and my former husband and I have made much happier lives for ourselves without each other as marriage partners.

It seems to me that the feminist issues in such phobias as mine are quite clearly related to various conflicts between dependence and independence. For example, the phobia of Connie, the young architect described in Chapter 4, expressed the conflict between guilt about not staying home all the time with her little girl and desire to go to work. Both Connie and I, like our own mothers, had problems separating from people we were close to (our daughters) and perhaps even exaggerated our "need" for them and their "need" for us. Our phobias solved the dilemma for each of us by making it appear as if we were too "sick" to do anything but stay home. I wanted to stay home anyway and finally chose work that permitted me to do this. Connie found through therapy that her daughter's "need" for her wasn't so great as Connie's "need" for her own mother seemed to be. Therefore there was no reason to feel guilty, and she could go back to work without fearing that she was harming her child (who, indeed, prospered).

Socialization contributes to the development of phobias in women in the sense that girls are taught that dependent behavior and attitudes of fearfulness and helplessness are part of a "feminine" image. Further, girls grow up expecting to be financially and emotionally supported by parentlike figures. When they are not, and often, as in my own case, even when they choose to support themselves, they may feel unconscious resentment that they aren't getting all that was "promised" to them. Some may convert their anger as well as their anxiety about their ability to take care of themselves into intense fearfulness, to the point where it appears as if the *fears* are preventing them from acting more autonomously. This is the usual function of phobias in women.

Phobias elicit a lot of attention because they arouse everyone's anxieties that his or her own fears (the kind everyone has) may break out in flamboyant ways. Phobias also can wreak all kinds of havoc on relationships, almost forcing a spouse or other family members to restrict their activities to the small area defined by the patient's fears or else suffer the guilt and tension engendered by not indulging the infantile demands of the phobic person. It is easy to see that phobias can be especially "useful" in some kinds of interpersonal conflicts, for one can use them to express resentment, to control the activities of others, and to express helplessness and dependency by making it appear that one needs unusual deference and protection. Phobias can also be used to draw attention away from real sources of anger and other tensions that family members, including the phobic person, may not want to confront directly.

A nonsexist philosophy can help prevent phobic reactions by encouraging men and women to develop attitudes of mutual interdependence in intimate relationships so that their needs for care and protection and for autonomy and self-realization can all be expressed. Feminism can be helpful in preventing phobias by changing girls' expectations that their future financial and emotional support will come mostly from sources outside themselves. When young women have confidence in their abilities to support and protect themselves and are provided by society with ways to do so, they will not be fearful or resentful of circumstances that require these capacities but will meet them with zest and skill.

The "Hysterical" Woman

Nothing seems to delight male doctors more than taking potshots at "hysterical" women in their professional literature. This is particularly true of psychotherapists, although other practitioners also look down upon "emotional" women from the heights of their obsessiveness. Our culture values most what men have learned: to keep oneself at a distance from feelings, to be "logical" as opposed to "emotional" in reasoning, to keep accurate accounts, to deliberate long and hard before making decisions, to pay attention to detail, and so on. Many women have learned a style of thinking and behaving that is in great contrast to the style of most "successful" men: impulsive, emotionally expressive, and easily "excitable" (aroused).

Our culture deplores such "childish" women, and men who value "self-control" above all other characteristics, often belittle women they see as "hysterical." There is not one case study in the psychological literature that is fair to a woman who falls into the "hysterical" classification.

Now, the irony of this is that it is exactly those men who pride themselves most on their "logic," their emotional control, and so on who are personally most drawn to the "hysterical" woman. And for good reason: She permits and facilitates emotionality in the man, and it is in her presence that he can get in touch with his feelings, particularly sexual excitement and tenderness. Indeed, men in our culture, especially those of the type to achieve success in the various intellectual disciplines and in the professions, may need as intimates and companions women whom, in their professional capacities, they might describe as "hysterical." Often, however, they choose to ignore their attraction to women of this type because they fear the intensity of the feelings aroused by them. The result of keeping themselves unaware of their own feelings is that they often select as wives women who are obsessive, like themselves, leaving their deepest emotional and sexual experiences to hurried extramarital encounters with women they feel they must not respect. Or such a man may marry a woman who excites him, only to feel and act superior to her for the rest of their lives, robbing both of them of true intimacy. "Hysterical" women go along with this put-down of themselves because they believe that the man is right. They have been told by their parents and teachers throughout their early lives that there is only one right and respectable way to be, and that is obsessive. When they get emotionally or physically sick they are reinforced in what they always knew: that the doctor is "right" and they, poor women, are wrong, even if only by virtue of the fact that the doctor got through medical school and they didn't.

I have a patient, a beautiful woman of twenty-one, who is a student in a philosophy class. Her teacher, a man of about forty-five, is constantly teasing her about her "illogical" mind. "You're overemotional," he says to her; "Why don't you learn to think?"; "You need to exercise some mental discipline"; and so on and so forth. All the while he is making these criticisms he looks down her dress or up her skirt and enjoys her ability to arouse him from the depths of his dispassion. She is insulted by his sadistic cracks, but she is also aroused by her ability—her power—to excite him. The same old story. The new twist would be if men were to truly respect these "emotional" women, which could happen only if they could respect and express their own emotionality rather than block it off. Can you imagine a doctor or professor admitting how much he needs and enjoys the "hysterical" women who are his patients, students, and associates and telling such a woman with love and respect how much she contributes to his pleasure in his work or his love life?

Obviously, no one personality style is "better" than any other, although one would never guess this from reading the psychological literature. Nowadays we can read the works of women and find the same contempt for men's obsessive cognitive and behavioral styles that they have had for our "hysterical" styles. This is pointless and self-defeating. Men and women can offer much to each other and should not have to be the same. The essentials are mutual respect and appreciation for what each contributes to the other's experience that they cannot supply for themselves. We will never be all things to ourselves any more than we can be all things to each other.

I think that hysteria may be more common in women than in men because women may have more "un-bound" psychic energy than men do. Women complain more often than men do about diffuse anxiety, diffuse excitement, and other emotions such as depression that they cannot relate to specific causes. Most women have very few focuses for their energy except Man, Home, and Family. That is one of the reasons some women overvalue these domestic involvements. The kind of work outside the home that has heretofore been available and acceptable to women cannot be compared to the professional challenges available to many men. The result is that many women feel emotionally disorganized, an extremely disagreeable sensation.

People who experience this kind of diffusion of emotionality try to put an end to it by all kinds of temporary distractions. Overeating is one of these. It reduces the anxiety of emotional disorganization by focusing the attention on a specific act and then on specific (if disagreeable) feelings, such as guilt and disgust. Very frequently people who have overeaten experience a relief of tension, which serves as a reward, often misinterpreted as the reward of ingesting comforting supplies. I think the reward is the reduction of tension that comes from focusing the emotions on something. That's why many people, especially "hysterics," who have trouble focusing energy anyway, eat when they are bored; they are simply supplying a focus, a structure, to some "unstructured" time. Another way the compulsive eater supplies a focus is by becoming involved with dieting, especially after he or she has just eaten too extravagantly. The pressure is off, for the moment, and a project can be envisioned: a project that has a long-term goal on which to focus. The problem is that the next time energy becomes uncomfortably disorganized (from anxiety, from anger, from excitement, from *anything!*) the quickest solution seems to be to focus on a short-term goal (get food and eat it).

There are many other ways that "hysterics" focus their energies. A notorious one is through the use of symptoms. Like obesity and dieting, a symptom can and often does become a *raison d'être*. Since all behavior is "overdetermined," it is impossible to say that this is the only reason people produce symptoms. Some of the others have been discussed in other chapters.

I think that more women will become "hysterical" if they cannot avail themselves of whatever opportunities are present for the organization of their considerable energies. And more opportunities need to be made available. Women are, of course, increasingly aware that Family and Home don't require the efforts they once did, and involvement in them will never again be so prestigious as it once was. Women need new goals worthy of their greatest efforts, and they need the training and confidence to seek them.

The major task of a therapist working with a "hysterical" woman is to help her discover how she stops herself from organizing her emotions and energies around interests that might absorb her and at the same time enhance her self-esteem. Usually I find that a woman who is focusing on temporary and possibly destructive "objects" or activities in an attempt to alleviate the anxiety that accompanies emotional diffusion is afraid of success, of happiness, of being a big person in the world, of challenge. Some women cannot believe that their success can "belong" to them; some women cannot accept an image of themselves as assertive; some women are afraid of competition. If there are opportunities available, therapy can be very useful in exploring and alleviating (where the patient desires this) the blocks to a rewarding, zestful, and focused work involvement.

Women's "Fidelity"

One of the qualities that is valued most highly in "good" women is loyalty, and loyalty in women is usually defined as sexual fidelity. Many women are outraged and frightened to learn that their husbands or lovers go to bed with other women when they believe themselves to be "faithful" to their men.

I know that my lover occasionally goes out with and sleeps with other women and is probably "unfaithful" to me in his fantasies many times a day, while I tell myself and him that I don't really enjoy being "unfaithful" to him (the other men I sleep with "don't count"). Obviously there are times when I like to think and want him to believe that he is getting more from me (I am more giving) than I get from him (he is more stingy).

Recently I had a shocking thought: Not only do I in fact occasionally enjoy going to bed with other men, but I am often nearly as intimate with my women friends as I am with my lover. He says he "needs" other women sexually because he, being a man, hasn't learned to be as intimate emotionally with his men friends as women can be with their women friends. He has to get into bed with someone before he can tell his secrets. Most of us women can do that over a cup of coffee, and we tell our female intimates the same secrets we let our lovers think we share only with them.

Absolute fidelity is a bullshit ideal, I've come to believe. It's too human to fall into bed with an attractive or even unattractive someone just because he or she is there and because, to be honest, one expects to have a good time making love. And then, as I say, there are our women friends, with whom we have cozy "affairs" all the time. Why is it, then, that some of us women hang onto this ridiculous notion of our "fidelity" while we bemoan the "promiscuity" of our closest male?

Women's Gossip About Men

Some women place great importance on men and at the same time fear them. Such women spend a greal deal of time talking to each other about the men in their lives. Much of this gossip is hostile and reflects something that I have named the comply-complain syndrome. When one person (often a member of an "outgroup") is afraid to confront another (particularly a member of an "in-group") with anger or dissatisfaction about their relationship or about some act of the other's, he or she may appear to comply with what's going on but may complain about it elsewhere.

For many reasons, probably chiefly because they are afraid of and angry with some men, certain women are sought out repeatedly by others to listen to and participate in bitching, which is what it is whether the words are gentle and subtle or strident and crude. Two or more women who are complaining about the men in their lives often have a feeling of pleasant camaraderie, the pseudo-intimate bond of conspirators. At the same time they may recognize that they are betraying not only their lovers but also themselves, for they may sense that they are keeping themselves from the experience of being able to share *all* of themselves with a lover. (Many serious infidelities, no matter what rationalizations are offered, result from the fear of sharing hostile or critical feelings with the person with whom one has a primary erotic relationship.)

It seems to me that women who engage in this kind of gossip about men are not "hostile women," nor are they women who are more hostile to men than to other women. They are more likely people who have learned to avoid conflict with another person whom they have made more important than themselves, and this may include the men they are involved with. It is not true, therefore, that women who go to consciousness-raising groups and bitch about the men they love and hate are necessarily bitchy women; they are women who have not yet learned to confront men with their anger or to be assertive about getting (or trying to get) what they want from men. If a consciousness-raising group serves no other function for women than providing a place for them to complain and get support for their feelings of anger and victimization, then it is not serving women's best interests. It is supplying only half of what women need. They also need to learn to engage in a real dialogue with their lovers (of either sex, by the way), or to choose new lovers with whom greater intimacy is possible.

Some people say they don't want intimacy; they say that they prefer to fragment their emotional involvements, satisfying this need with this one, that need with that one. A therapist is suspicious, but it's a free country.

Occasionally a feminist therapist will fall into the trap of listening to a female patient's complaints about the man in her life and even supporting the woman against the man, a person whom the therapist may never have met. In most relationships there are no absolute villains and no absolute victims. There are two or more people engaged in some sort of system, each contributing behavior that keeps the system going. When listening to angry or victimized feelings expressed by one party to a complex interaction, a therapist may want to ask: "Why are you telling me this? What are your fantasies about how I will reply?" These and similar questions should alert the patient that the therapist is not up for a coffee klatch or for a conspiracy of women against men or even for the kind of intimacy that the patient may expect will follow the old seductive ploy of setting up a common enemy.

"Nonsexist Childrearing"

Every couple of decades there appears a new formula for the development of ideologically pure children. These never work because children are supposed to turn out to be the opposite of what their parents want them to be. The more emphasis a parent puts on one value system, the more likely it is that the child will turn out to represent exactly what the parent has tried to stamp out of him or her.

Nonsexist childrearing is great in theory, but it won't work unless it's demonstrated in the parents' lives. If the mother works and can stand up for herself, her daughter is more likely to grow up to do the same than if the opposite is true, no matter how many storybooks the child reads about mothers who are firepersons or doctors or heads of households.

I never read or bought my daughter anything merely because I thought it would be "good" for her. She reads whatever appeals to her and manipulates me into buying toys that she likes to play with, even Barbie dolls. I realize that I "shouldn't" let her do that, just as I shouldn't allow her to eat so many potato chips, but the fact is that I don't want to spend all my time hovering over her, fretting about her values and her health. She isn't going to be perfect anyway, and neither am I going to be the perfect mother. A rationalization, no doubt, but it is inconceivable to me that she will grow up to be a passive, frightened, inferior-feeling woman, no matter how many dolls and how few trucks she plays with. There are simply no important models in her life who fit that description.

When a Feminist Therapist Works with Men

I have a number of male patients who certainly did not come to me because they had heard that I am concerned with feminist issues in psychotherapy. Most male patients come to a feminist therapist because they are referred by women in their lives who are already patients or because they have heard that the therapist is competent.

I can't speak for the feelings of other feminist therapists who work with men, so let me say how it is for me. I think one of my biggest problems in treating male patients, and a problem for them too, is that I am especially drawn to somewhat passive, gentle men who like to be made comfortable. I can feel motherly and sexual toward men like this aged two to eighty as long as they are not too passively angry or withdrawn to respond appreciatively. Such men often do not demonstrate the aggressiveness of the male-chauvinist types, but that may cause difficulties for them, and the feminist therapist who responds positively to the unassertiveness of a male patient because she approves of his behavior ideologically may not be helping him much.

Ironically, then, with some male patients I have to be particularly alert to support their "masculine" characteristics, whereas this is not so much a problem for me with women, since I tend to respond more positively to assertive women than to passive women.

Usually I ask a new male patient why he has come to a woman therapist and what some of his fears are about seeing a feminist. Often he will express some anxiety that I may be prejudiced against him just because he's a man, and we talk about his fantasies, projections, and so on. It's vital to do this because every man in our culture has learned *some* prejudice against women. He may somewhere in the back of his mind doubt my professional competence; he may fear that I will try to "castrate" him (if he sees professional women as particularly aggressive); and so on. These are all stereotypes about women that he has absorbed in some way from the culture, and it is important that he recognize them and feel free to share them with the therapist. On her part, the female therapist needs to have worked through her own anger at men's prejudices toward women to the extent that, even if she expresses this anger at a moment when her patient seems to insult or patronize her, she can still use her emotions to help the patient and not to destroy his self-esteem or assert her moral "superiority."

I feel very strongly that if a therapist dislikes a patient and the patient's main orientation to life, then the therapist shouldn't work with this person. If a feminist therapist can't stand any expression of a male patient's learned sexism then she'd better not work with him, for if that is an important part of his self-image, he's not going to be able to change it without anxiety. All therapists need to be understanding of their patients' anxieties about change, even when these anxieties are expressed in hostile ways. But the therapist cannot extend such understanding if she is so threatened by the patient's hostility that she can't think straight. The therapist must therefore be able to communicate not only understanding of the patient's feelings but also something of her own anxiety. We can ask our patients to understand us, too!

Love, Sex, and the Women's Movement

How the women's movement is now affecting and will in the future affect love relationships and the meaning of "love" to women are absorbing questions. By now everyone has heard someone say that women's new assertiveness and independence are "causing" an increase in male impotence. This is an absolutely groundless accusation. Large numbers of people of both sexes have sexual problems of one kind or another, and these problems are *never* exclusively the fault of the partner's behavior. It is vitally important that both partners feel entitled to sexual pleasure and that each take responsibility for communicating what he or she desires in order to experience pleasure. If the communication is made and the partner repeatedly cannot or will not comply, then obviously the one who is frustrated needs to assess the feasibility of finding a more willing lover or suggesting sex therapy or psychotherapy for them as a couple.

The women's movement can help women to experience more sexual pleasure by freeing them from their old inhibitions about communicating their sexual needs and revealing their arousal and orgasms. In addition, the liberated woman will value herself as much as she does her lover and consequently will cherish and seek her own satisfaction as she cherishes and tries to provide for his.

If a woman uses her new self-assertiveness just to be hostile to or accusing of her lover, he may, of course, "turn off," but even this is not exclusively her fault, for he may have provoked her anger or be unable to tell her to shove those hostile messages. If he himself cannot be assertive or cannot maintain his self-esteem in the face of her anger, that is his problem. They both have a problem if they insist on making love while either partner is feeling hostile or anxious. If a man feels that his lover is angry and tries to make love anyway, only to find he can't get it up, how is it the woman's "fault"? Who made him do it?

This brings me to another important issue. The feminist movement has provided a vehicle for the direct expression of a great deal of hostility by women toward men. Men are often scapegoated by feminists as the "cause" of women's problems just as parents were, until recently, scapegoated as the "causes" of their children's psychological difficulties. (My mother told me when I was an unhappy adolescent that I couldn't go to a psychotherapist because, she said, "They teach you to hate your parents." I suppose some men must be afraid that their wives' or lovers' feminist therapists may teach them to hate men. I hope this isn't true.)

If the women's movement encourages a woman to assert her rights where previously she was unable to and to express anger where it is appropriate, this is a good thing. But if a woman is hostile toward men in general or denies that men have rights, too, her hostility existed and was expressed in some way long before the modern feminist movement. Feminism need not and should not be synonymous with hatred or distrust of men. As I indicated in Chapter 1, men and women alike are harmed by sex-role stereotyping, and both can benefit from "consciousness raising."

There is no more difficult challenge in life than that of relating intimately, sexually and emotionally to another human being over a sustained period of time. It's certainly tempting, but beside the point entirely, to blame these difficulties solely on the behavior we have learned as men and women. Even without masculine-feminine myths and sex-role stereotyping, love would be immensely complex and full of disappointments (in ourselves and in the other). Indeed, in spite of the apparent destructive influence of women's socialization, women are probably better able to give and receive love than men are. I think women care more about love than men do, and I think women get more out of love.

A man and a woman can never have a loving relationship if they cannot, first of all, grieve together that many of their fantasies about themselves as a couple, about themselves as individuals, and about "love" will never come true. Many of these fantasies are not related to sex-role learning. The mutual expression of their fantasies and mourning for their loss should help lovers liberate themselves from the horrors of blaming their own and the other's gender for love's inevitable disappointments.

For example, all lovers want to own the loved person and, at the same time, yearn to escape from the other's possessiveness. These submerged wishes need to be acknowledged, respected, and dealt with as human, yet impossible of fulfillment. Another fantasy we all share as lovers, from time to time, is the desire to be rescued (or to rescue the other) from "bad" feelings such as self-hatred, depression, anxiety, and confusion. The wish to be rescued by another or to rescue another from himself needs to be recognized along with its futility. Another fantasy: all of us unconsciously and occasionally even consciously make the demand that the loved one supply for us those parts of ourselves that we have split off or never acquired. Where a lover can comfortably "complement" us, this is great, but the stunning fact is, to paraphrase Fritz Perls, that we are not here to complete each other. We are simply here. *We need to be aware of our demand* in order to let the other off the hook and either let go of our own unsatisfied hunger or supply what we want for ourselves. These are only a few of the fantasies that distort and disturb love relationships yet are probably not related to gender.

Feminism can contribute positively to a woman's love life by helping her to find new sources of self-esteem and new opportunities for personal growth; it can support a woman in getting what she wants from a cooperative man and in leaving one who is unwilling or unable to help her realize herself romantically and sexually; it can support her self-esteem and therefore her self-assertion and courage in finding a new lover, or in deciding not to have a lover at all, if that is what she prefers.

I suspect I differ from some other feminists in my belief that the importance women place on loving may be a good thing. Picasso said, "Love is a great refreshment." It is that, and more. Satisfying love can be a great enhancement to the self, a source of pleasure and excitement, and a powerful motivation for keeping oneself healthy enough to live and love forever. But it cannot be any of these things if it is not given importance in the psyche. Nor can love be good for women if they value men more than themselves. Love should not be taken lightly (although it should also not be taken only seriously). Whatever contributes to a woman's happiness in loving is good for her; whatever is good for women must be feminist.

A question often asked is whether the women's movement has "caused" an increase in lesbianism. My answer is that there is certainly a relationship between the two but not one that is directly causal except insofar as feminist organizations and meetings may provide opportunities for lesbian women to meet and be turned on to each other. Feminism is one of many contemporary liberation movements that support the questioning of old assumptions regarding human interaction. Inevitably, some of those assumptions have to do with sexual mores, and thus there is an increase in experimentation with all kinds of new behaviors among the supporters of radical movements.

The "public" seems to associate lesbianism and feminism partly out of anxious hostility toward feminists. Thus one hears "Only a lesbian would be a feminist." Actually, every new or offbeat political movement has been accused of encouraging or supporting people who engage in unconventional sexual behavior. People who are anxious about the liberation of women (or any new idea) try hard to believe that its supporters are crazy, hostile to the dominant group, or at least unappealing to or uninterested in the dominant group. In distorted, anxious minds, lesbians (like hippies) embody all three of these characteristics. Of course many lesbians are not feminists, nor are most of them particularly hostile toward or unattractive to men. It is absurd to think that a woman becomes a lesbian simply because she is hostile to men. By this logic, women love men because they are hostile to women.

Will more women become lesbian as more women are influenced by feminism? Yes, because more women will be brave enough to do whatever they want to do and that may well include loving other women sexually. It's possible that the feminists' support of women's closeness to each other will provide an opportunity for some women to discover that they prefer homosexual love, but this is not to say that feminism causes lesbianism. Nobody knows what "causes" anyone to become homosexual, but it is certainly more complicated than the influence of a particular social movement. My Aunt Sayde used to say that her (Jewish) son became a Catholic priest because he was influenced by the University of Chicago. Can it be?

Love and Women's Creativity

Like many women, I once felt that I "needed" to be loved and encouraged by a man whom I respected and loved before I could feel worthwhile enough to express myself in any particularly creative or unique way. Many women want things from a man that only they can give themselves, such as self-respect and a fuller sense of themselves. But since they can never get these things from outside themselves they are often frustrated and angry with the man for not giving "enough."

The problem for most women is not to "get" enough but to "be" enough. In order to feel fulfilled, we must no longer hold back from ourselves and from others in our lives the "best" and the "worst" aspects of our personalities.

For example, it is very common for intelligent women to suppress their competence and their discernment because competence may lift them above the crowd, where they would be vulnerable to critical attention as well as to charges of "immodesty," and because they then risk seeing themselves as women whom no man may want to protect. In addition, discernment puts critical eyes back into their own heads, and too often they are afraid to see, much less disclose, the flaws in those whose support they think they need. Many women would identify as the "worst" in themselves their angry, bitchy, self-interested feelings and behavior. They would prefer to hold onto an image of themselves as rather flat emotionally but pleasant and nice. Suppressing so much of themselves, many women naturally sense that they are incomplete and look for completion—everywhere but in the right place. They thus experience themselves as "needing" rather than the more assertive "wanting," and thereby feel themselves to be more helpless than they really are.

The great struggle to recognize and to express the "best" and the "worst" of themselves is one that involves all women who want to feel like whole persons rather than like dolls or Victorian children. Perhaps women in love and women who are engaged in creative work feel this struggle most poignantly because it is in these very arenas that they have been urged to be very careful of how they present themselves. Learning to be authentic in love and in creative work can be difficult for everyone, but it is especially so for members of stigmatized groups, for they are too ready to comply with others' expectations of them in order to forestall disapproval and rejection.

I now interpret the connection between my love life and my creative life differently, having myself negotiated some of the struggle I mentioned. I no longer feel that my creative output is dependent on my lover's support and approval. (As a matter of fact, I can seriously question with him his "need" to serve that function for me.) It seems to me now that because both our relation-

ship and my writing engage me at the level of my deepest
feelings (the best and the worst!) I experience a connection between the two. Both involvements seem to organize energy that I sense as my most complete and exciting
self.

I believe that there is something fundamentally erotic
about creativity, and in this respect I agree with Freud.
However, I do not believe, as Freud did, that creativity is
a "sublimation," a conversion of libidinal energy. To me,
being able to create is the result of feeling free to be in
love with and to celebrate the self. It is the same energy
and the same process with which one is in love with and
celebrates a lover. I have noticed that most patients who
seem blocked creatively and in their love lives experience
shameful feelings about some aspects of themselves that
at the same time they long to reveal. How typical this is of
women's history! Perhaps there is a relationship between
this aspect of their histories and many women's lack of
fulfillment in both love and creativity.

Sex and Anger: Women's "Secrets"

In my family when I was growing up, open expression
of sexual or angry feelings and behavior was considered
appropriate only to the criminally insane, crude little
boys, and poor people. Like most little girls, I wanted
desperately to be seen as sane (legitimate), ladylike, and
loving, but at the same time I knew, as we all know about
ourselves, that I was not really all of these things or even
any of them for longer than a few minutes at a time. I
thought I had to keep my "badness" a secret, and I
developed a consuming passion to learn whether others
had similar secrets. I relentlessly asked "personal" questions of my parents' friends; I was interested in any
information about them that my own parents would

never have revealed about themselves, such as how old they were, what their "real" feelings were about their husbands, wives, children, and servants, and how much money they had. The answers to any of these questions if I was lucky enough to get them seemed like invaluable treasure to me, and apparently they still do, for I'm still avidly asking the same questions, and more!

Although I must suppose that my parents' attitudes toward sex were destructive, no oppression could ever have stamped out my sexuality, because I found that during adolescence the best way to learn people's secrets is to sleep with them. Later on one can be a therapist. I am luckier, however, than many women who learned that even as married adults they must hide their capacities for sensual pleasure from their partners and, most destructively, from themselves. Too many women are no longer in touch with their eroticism at all and, like my patient Lenore, are so threatened by the prospect of awakening their sexuality that they prefer to shut themselves off completely from anything that would remind them that they are sexual beings.

What affected me most adversely as a girl was my family's illusion that nice girls (indeed, all nice people) didn't have and certainly didn't reveal hostile feelings. Although I was in many respects a normally nasty little girl, I always felt extremely guilty about my bad temper and "selfish" behavior. Only recently have I been able to experience my average nasty self without feeling that I must produce, along with the awareness of my hostility, punishments such as headaches, rashes, and fatness.

Most people in middle-class society have trouble letting themselves be "unpleasant" without guilt. We forget that everyone has hostile feelings and that it is unnecessary as well as futile to try to protect our associates from them, since these feelings will find expression in some way. There is little doubt that women have been cajoled even more than men to be "nice," to be quiet, to "sit down and don't get excited, dear." Such "nice" people of both sexes get cancer, strokes, migraine, and often become overwhelmingly depressed or explosively violent. The only woman I have ever known who made it a guiding principle of her life never to suppress her anger or meanness is my grandmother, whom I have described before. At ninety-six she is still going strong, I think entirely on hostility. She has never been sick and has never looked less than gorgeous, fully groomed and gowned at all hours of the day and night. Of course she is so unpleasant that nobody wants to go near her, but is she healthy!

Contrary to what most people believe, anger openly acknowledged and expressed doesn't wreck intimate relationships nearly so often as anger repressed or denied. When anger cannot be recognized and given legitimacy, conflicts cannot be resolved, and unresolved conflicts sap energy and dull the capacity to feel pleasurable excitement. Probably more women's sex lives are ruined by repressed hostility than by repressed sexuality. In middle-class American society it may be more a confirmation of genuine intimacy between two lovers if they feel free to be angry with each other than if they merely feel free to fuck each other!

11

Conclusion

I've just been reading of the passage by France's National Assembly of a liberalized abortion law for that conservative Roman Catholic country. Obviously many Western women are already experiencing great progress in being able to choose their own roles in life rather than having these roles thrust upon them by Nature or presumably outside forces. (I say *presumably* because it is hard for a therapist to believe that except in unusual cases a woman is entirely a "victim" of pregnancy—or much else, for that matter.)

The subjects of pregnancy and abortion stir many memories and thoughts in me relevant to the basic issues of this book. In the Preface I suggested that new choices of identities, roles, and life-styles would bring many women into conscious or unconscious conflict with the deeply invested lifelong roles and values around which their emotional lives have to a great extent been organized. For many women these cannot be disturbed or repudiated without turmoil, pain, anxiety, and grief. I believe it is one of the most important functions of the therapist to help all people who are considering fundamental changes in their sex-role expectancies and other learned behaviors to anticipate fully the feelings that may accompany these changes, not the least of which may well be some mourning for a renounced part of one's being. It may be that only after this difficult emotional "labor" will the ego feel the deepest joys of liberation. It is *not* appropriate for a therapist to help a patient deny the former importance of her older values by rationalizing away their earlier significance in her life or by advancing new ideologies without regard for what these may mean for this particular patient.

Few feminist writers or therapists pay sufficient attention to the depth of feeling that accompanies role-expectancies. The deep desire to be a wife or a mother, for example, may indeed be learned from the culture, but this does not make it a superficial aspect of the self; on the contrary. All of our deepest convictions are learned or "culturally conditioned." Throughout history and certainly even today, some brave people have chosen to give up their lives rather than betray their most profound beliefs, for to them betrayal of these deep (and *learned*) aspects of the self would be experienced as tantamount to the death of the self.

I am a modern, educated, sophisticated, self-supporting, "liberated" woman. Besides, I am beyond the time of life and far from living a style of life that would make pregnancy desirable, nor do I want another child. Yet last night I dreamed I was pregnant.

Twenty-five years ago, almost exactly as I write this, I was pregnant. I was eighteen and unmarried. I lived in a city where my family was well known, and I was completing my first year at a prestigious college. A very old human story. If it were happening today the pressure to have a now readily attainable abortion would probably be irresistible, but in those days having an illegal abortion was almost as scary and sordid as having an illegitimate baby. Besides, I wanted desperately to have a child—a "learned" value, certainly, but a very real one. My mother urged me to have an abortion and went so far as to arrange one without my knowledge, with a doctor in another town.

In spite of the potential social rejection and humiliation, to which I was very sensitive, my "need" to be a mother provided me with a strength of purpose that I now see as really extraordinary, since my mother was and still is a most aggressive and convincing lady. (My recurrent dream in those months was of the sturdy, strongminded woman who was my mother carrying the fetus off in a paper bag.) In spite of my mother and my own anxiety and guilt I persisted in hanging on to my baby, and hasty wedding arrangements were transacted. Needless to say, even after I was "decently" married, no one was deceived about the circumstances of my son's conception. Somehow I knew that I could and must transcend the disgrace and the shame, which I felt in marked degree, especially in relation to my parents, and that I would go on to prove that in spite of what they and others said, I was neither a bad nor a self-destructive person, nor was I being stupid or hysterical.

Oddly enough, even though my choice was "nonrational" and my drive to be a mother was nonfeminist, having that baby was one of the best things I ever did for myself, as valuable as any of my "rational" or "feminist" choices. Becoming a mother helped to integrate my personality in a way that was essential to my mental health at the time. Motherhood, even at nineteen, did not interfere with my intellectual growth or prevent me from realizing my career goals; it simply was not, as so many feminists say, destructive to my self-fulfillment. It was a vital part of my self-fulfillment and still is.

The reason I tell this story is to point out that while the modern woman is certainly entitled to free choice of role changes and of new identities, she should realize that not choosing a once valued role in the service of a new ideology may also bring her pain. If a patient of mine, married or not, is pregnant and wants an abortion, the feminist position—that she is entitled not to be a mother and is a worthwhile person even if she chooses this course—is obviously not the only one to consider. She now has the freedom to choose abortion, but the fact that the option exists and seems expedient and "sensible" at the moment doesn't mean it is the decision that will make her happiest. A woman shouldn't have to feel guilty for wanting to live out an "old-fashioned" role.

I believe that the feminist movement can help women to negotiate their traditional roles more effectively as well as to consider, choose, and function in new roles. This seems to me to be an important part of what freedom is all about and what change is all about. Certainly we need to have divorce counseling and abortion counseling and career counseling. We need also to provide help for women of all ages and classes who want to be mothers, wives, nurses, and housekeepers.

Women can do *both* if they want to: live out older roles happily and find fulfillment in new ones. Not everyone may be able to accomplish these simultaneously, but women have always been geniuses at organization, and most of them will, if given encouragement and support, find ways to combine the old and the new, if that is what they want. I hope that therapists who work with contemporary women will help them to recognize all aspects of their many selves and will not encourage them to split off parts of themselves without at least experiencing, with profound awareness and emotion, what the loss may mean. It has never been the goal of psychotherapy merely to make people's lives pain-free or more efficient. Self-awareness in order to make the most meaningful choices and in order to experience a fully integrated self must be the major goal of all therapies, including feminist therapy.

Index